Published in the United States by FourCats Press
ISBN: 978-1-7320442-8-9
Library of Congress Control Number: 2020930037

Book design by FourCats Press
First FourCats Press Edition: January 2020
www.FourCatsPress.com
Editor@FourCatsPress.com

HOW TO READ A PHOTOGRAPH

Frame & Focus

Carolyn Whitson

First Edition

FOURCATS PRESS

2020

TABLE OF CONTENTS

The act of photographic interpretation relies on how much knowledge a viewer brings to an image. If the photo is of a particular genre, such as photojournalism or street photography, then a person's knowledge of the place or people photographed, or of the work of famous street photographers, will contribute greatly to an understanding of what is being shown in the image. If the genre of photography is landscape, portraiture, or abstract photography, the degree of a person's knowledge of art and art history can significantly influence what she/he gets out of an image. Because most people in the West have lived their lives inundated with photography through advertisement, magazines, television, and film, and the majority of us will own some sort of camera in our lifetime, and even appear in photos ourselves, we already have embedded within us a significant understanding of how to read a photograph, though we may never have encountered the vocabulary for expressing that understanding.

This book seeks to give you that vocabulary and a procedure for reading a photograph. It is difficult to notice things deeply for which we don't have words and, with the vocabulary here, my hope is that you can notice in much more detail how photos are composed, what elements make some more compelling to you than others, and why photos have the power to affect how you interpret things you see outside their frames. While this book trains your eyes in reading photographs, it will also reveal how photos have trained your eyes to see objects in the world.

Think of the camera as having three sides instead of just the usual two. We have the photographer on one side of the camera, looking through the lens to frame a subject for exposure; we also have the subject who (if a person) has consented (we hope) to be framed in the photo. As well, we have the audience or viewer, who views the finished product of that interactive moment among photographer, camera, and subject.

The placement of the viewer on the third "side" of the camera is a philosophical one. In thinking of the power dynamics of a photographic moment, the viewer can be said to be about as passive as the subject, consenting to see as the subject has consented to be seen. Or the viewer can be on the same side as the photographer, bringing personal knowledge and desires as a point-of-view and taking what s/he wants from the image. Both the photographer and viewer interpret the subject, but the photographer gets there first and creates the conditions under which the subject is seen.

I suggest we place the viewer either above or below the camera for that third side. This is also a philosophical stance: being separated by time from the action of creating the photo, viewers may feel that the image exists above and beyond them, with its own untouchable reality and ultimate meaning. Or viewers may feel above the photo, considering it an object that is completely within their control to see as they please. The viewer is part of a triad in the making of a photo (the camera constrains all three players), but the viewer's disposition and powers of interpretation can change with the more she or he knows about photography and the subject. Your knowledge and interest as a viewer will determine how close or far, how engaged or detached, how clear or confused you are when you look at a photo.

The concepts I give here for understanding photos are by no means exhaustive, but they should be enough for you to be able to articulate quite clearly what is in the composition of a photo and to argue about which elements are compelling for you. My hope is that, with this knowledge, you'll be able to look more critically at photos presented to you and gain a little analytic distance from photos that are put in front of you in order to manipulate your perceptions of reality.

What is more, I want you to have some tools for understanding how a photo moves you to think or feel in a particular way. For those of you who are photographers, I hope the concepts help you to develop your own skills and to articulate aspects of your work that you like or want to improve.

 After the concepts are covered in this text, there is a section that provides you with an organized checklist for coordinating the concepts as you arrive at a decisive analysis. We'll work through examples to help you develop your critical eye and to reinforce what you've learned in reading. I've tried to model some of this analysis in my explanations of the photos I've used to illustrate the various concepts. Please refer to them if you find yourself at a loss to articulate what you're seeing.

   Appreciating photos can lead you into a lifetime of enjoying them as art and into understanding how individuals and groups use photos to unite and divide. Whatever your desired outcome in reading photos, I hope this book helps you reach your goals.

▼ *Romanesque Capital* (Conques, France)

Understanding these key concepts in photo analysis will take you deeper into understanding and open doors for your own photography. The vocabulary provided here will give you a means to articulate what you see in photographs, helping you to express your analysis of an image with clarity and precision. The old saying goes, "I don't know much about art, but I know what I like." My goal for you here is for you to know enough about art (and the technical aspects of photography) that you can understand and express precisely what makes a photo compelling to you.

Image/Photo

With the advent of digital photography, the definition of a photo or image has changed in subtle but significant ways. Where one could once encapsulate the meaning of this term with a description of what a print and a negative are, most images now exist as files. Within those files are not just the recording of how light hit a sensor at a particular moment, but also all the metadata of the image's existence: the camera settings, the photographer's copyright, the geotagging of where the photo was taken, and more. A file can hold a record of alterations made to it, which may be significant for understanding the artist's techniques and can also provide clues to how "authentic" an image might be as a record of some reality.

For the audience of a photograph, what exists is what the viewer can see. In the days when film was the main recorder of images, that visual information was printed somewhere on some sort of paper and on the negative (or, in some cases, the positive). Now most images exist on a screen, and the settings of the screen itself can alter what the audience sees.

In this text, "image" and "photo" are used interchangeably. You should understand them as the description of a two-dimensional visual display that is derived from a camera and presented for viewing in a defined framework.

Once a photo has been processed and released for viewing by a photographer or editor, the image is available for reading and interpretation. For our purposes, a photo exists when it is viewed, and the act of viewing imbues the photo with meanings that an audience can interpret.

Romanesque Capital (Conques, France) meets the definition of a photo or image. It is a recording of how light hit a particular subject as it was framed by the camera. Many things can be said that would deepen this basic description of the photo and lead to better understanding, but we start with the most essential thing that can be said about it.

Frame

A frame is the boundary of a photographic image. Framing matters because it guides the eye, pointing to what is significant in the photo and sometimes suggesting what is outside a photo. The frame directs and contains the viewer's attention. Through framing, the photo becomes a contained unit that encloses a subject for the viewer to discern and consider. Containment can suggest that an image is whole and complete, though sometimes photographers will "break the frame" to imply the world or a subject outside of what they have presented for viewing. Such a breakage can jar the viewer into thinking about the subject beyond what is shown.

3

Solomon's Seal, Minnesota is contained within a frame—the boundaries of the photograph—that draws especial attention to the berries of the plant and the texture of the leaves. The framing is an authorial choice of the photographer, who has opted to emphasize the geometric qualities of the plant rather than adopt the more journalistic perspective that could be achieved by pulling back to include the whole plant in the image. The frame here holds nothing in completeness except the berries: all of the leaves are cut off by the frame. Still, there is enough detail that the viewer can infer the rest of each leaf from what is included. Given the centrality of the berries, and their greater visual weight in the image, the leaves themselves act as a frame-within-a-frame for the berries as the subject.

▲ *Solomon's Seal, Minnesota*
Panther on Etruscan Vase, Getty Villa, California ▶

Focus

The term focus has two different meanings in analyzing a photograph. One is the broad sense, in which it is used to describe what is emphasized within the photo by its framing, lighting, and visual weight. The other, more technical sense speaks to where the camera created the greatest sharpness in the frame. Certain genres of photography value sharp focus more than others: photojournalism, which emphasizes a truth-telling intention; documentary/scientific photography, which seeks to portray a subject with as much objectivity as possible; or macrophotography, in which special lenses create a very shallow depth of field for focus in order to bring some element in the frame very sharply into view.

In documenting an object for academic purposes, such as the detail of a vase in *Panther on Etruscan Vase, Getty Villa, California*, sharpness and larger-than-life scale are the expectation. They give the viewer access to the smallest details of the piece such as, in this image, the incisions made into the pottery to create emphasis and contrast in the panther, something the painting technology of the time could not create.

The raindrops and leaf details in *Fern in the Rain, Minnesota* are in perfect focus only along the left-of-center portion of the frame. But their clarity makes for an arresting quality in a photograph with so many spots of high and low contrast.

The softness of the cat's fur and the low lighting in *Enkidu in Soft Focus* made a sharp focus hard to attain (not to mention that animal subjects are rarely still for more than a fraction of a second, making sharp exposures in low light difficult to manage). The details in his pupils, whiskers, and nose suggest that this subject is in focus, but the overall quality of the image is quite soft.

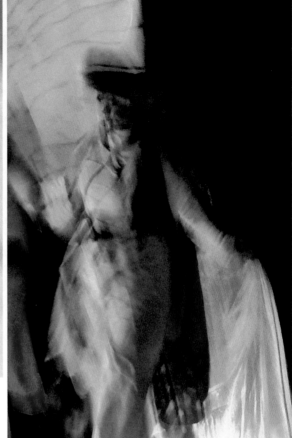

▲ *Enkidu in Soft Focus*   *Clothed, Descending a Staircase* ▶

◀ *Fern in the Rain, Minnesota*

Fine-art photography can take license with sharpness to create dramatic effects, as is seen in the impressionistic style of the photograph of a dancer (*Clothed, Descending a Staircase*). Arguably, the subject's face is in focus, or is at least discernible but, in fact, nothing here is "tack sharp," as photographers call it. If the goal had been to take a personal portrait of this subject, this photo might be termed a failure because her facial and bodily details are blurred to the point that she can't be confidently identified. The blur caused by her movements in low light, however, and the way this image evokes both impressionist paintings and modernist ones (particularly Duchamp's famous Modernist painting, *Nude Descending a Staircase*), give this photo other reasons for being pleasing to study, and so it works well.

Bokeh

Bokeh is a Japanese term for the quality of the out-of-focus portions of a photo and is usually used by photographers to compare lenses in how they render those portions. For our purposes, bokeh is the out-of-focus area of an image which frames the subject, contributing to the aesthetic beauty of the composition. (The word is pronounced "bo-kay," although people differ on how forcefully to pronounce the second syllable; in general, it shouldn't sound exactly like the word

▲ *Whoosh!*   *Bleeding Hearts* ▼

"bouquet.") Bokeh can either call attention to itself or be so smooth that it becomes an unremarkable background.

In *Whoosh!*, you can tell that, behind the butterfly, are shrubs and leaves, but they are so blurred as to be indeterminate. They frame the butterfly and highlight how it seems to hang in space. The flowers in the background are also rendered smooth, but they are not so blurred that you cannot identify them as the same type of flowers as those that are visible in the foreground. The difference between the sharply-focused flowers and the blurred ones creates a pleasing effect in the frame.

In the photo of the bleeding heart plant (*Bleeding Hearts*), the bokeh provides a striking contrast to the pink flowers. The lawn behind the flowers is hit so brightly by the sun that it registers as a light source itself. You can see circles of light behind the flowers, sometimes called "bokeh balls." These give you an idea of the details of the lens used. The closer to perfectly round the bokeh balls are, the more blades the lens had (in this case, nine). What you are seeing is the size and shape of the aperture when the light hit the camera's sensor.

The bokeh in an image can give you an idea of how narrow the depth of field is in a shot. In *Chicken Wire*, a rather abstract photo of a bale of chicken wire being unrolled, the in-focus part of the roll is in the middle plane of the image. The wire in the foreground blurs into a bokeh that is still recognizable as chicken wire but which makes the wire into hazy hexagons. The greenery in the background is so blurred that you can't distinguish the plants with any certainty, but notice that it is more blurred than the foreground, even though both are out of focus in the same part of the image. They are not equally out of focus, so the bokeh, even though it is a blur, represents two different depths in the frame.

Depth of Field

Depth of field refers to the degree of sharp focus in a photo, suggesting three-dimensionality of the items in a frame. As discussed in other definitions, macrophotography often features a very shallow depth of field because of the design constraints of a lens that can photograph something small at larger than a 1:1 ratio. Our binocular vision helps us to perceive the three dimensions of the world and navigate within space. Most cameras have only one lens and translate their exposure onto a two-dimensional surface, though newer cellphone cameras have two lenses that combine central elements in focus and impose them on another that is completely out of focus in order to create a

Chicken Wire ▶

portrait effect). Photographers can stage photos to suggest three dimensions in a two-dimensional plane by choosing to shoot with a small aperture, using a lens with strong subject separation that resists compression of objects behind the subject in a frame, and by physically positioning the camera to highlight objects as distinct in space.

Rievaulx Abbey uses the repeating rhythm of the ruined passage of the building to suggest great depth. As viewers, television and movies have trained us to understand that smaller things in a two-dimensional image are farther away than larger things. In this image, the crescent arches in the lower third of the frame are smaller and narrower than the same shapes in the top of the frame. The crescents diminish in size proportionally, and this creates a telescoping effect, which we've also come to understand as reflecting long-distance perspective. Most importantly here, the items are in focus as sharply in the foreground as in the background, which gives the viewer the ability to study the entire image as the subject. A shallow depth of field, in contrast, would incline the viewer to concentrate on only the sharpest parts of the image.

The clay mask in *Medusa Mask, Montepulciano, Italy* is in the foreground and in focus. Behind it, though, the bas-relief plaques are blurry, and the grain of the wood floor becomes indistinct. This photo can be said to have a fairly shallow depth of field. The lens used and the aperture selected for the exposure created a fairly clear separation of subject: the snakes of the Medusa pull away from the surrounding elements to suggest they are in the foreground.

The separation of subject is especially noticeable in the empty eye-sockets. The rims of the eyes are in sharp detail and, because the wood grain visible through the sockets is less distinct, the eyes convey a fraction of an inch of depth.

An especially sharp, deep depth of field gives an image a journalistic or scientific atmosphere. The crispness of details encourages the viewer to look closely to examine multiple layers of information. A shallow

10

Rievaulx Abbey ▶

depth of field can create a dreamier, more fine-arts aspect to an image. In *God of Peace*, a very large Art Deco statue (the subject of the shot reflected on the mirrored ceiling) is in sharp focus, but all the other elements of the architecture that surround the statue are so far away and dimly lit that they fade into nearly indistinct forms. The image here can confuse the eye because the camera actually photographed a flat surface (tilted at a bit of a slope because I was positioned near the ceiling but couldn't shoot at a ninety-degree angle), but the subject in the reflection is three-dimensional. The relationship of the body and face of the statue in space is preserved on the mirrors' surfaces, but the camera read the image as light hitting an angled 2D surface.

The degree of depth of field in a photo can give you clues about theme and mood. While it is easy to dismiss an image with full depth-of-field as "just reality," it is in fact an artistic choice of the photographer to guide the reader to particular responses. Awareness of how depth of field affects the composition of a photo can help refine your analysis.

◤ *Medusa Mask, Montepulciano, Italy*
God of Peace ▶

Visual Weight

Objects in a photographic frame can be discussed in terms of how their relationship works in balance with each other. When one part of an image draws more attention to the eye because of its greater size, its key lighting, its sharpness of focus, or its color intensity, it can be said to have "visual weight." If one object pulls more visual weight than others in the frame, it might be termed the dominant or subject of the photo because the eye keeps returning to it as that eye travels around the frame.

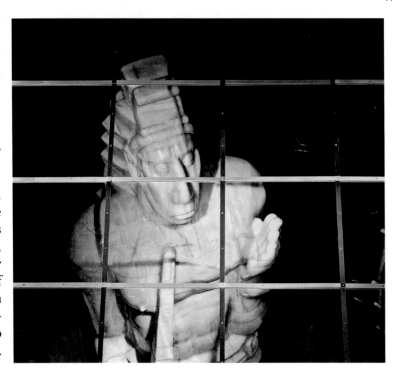

In *The Kid Stays in the Picture, Lowry Bridge, Minneapolis*, the child has more visual weight because her coat provides the highest contrast in the photo and its color is the most saturated. Though the bridge and buildings are larger, and the body of water traverses the whole frame, she is in the foreground and breaks from the essentially geometric character of the rest of the image.

The flamingo taking a drink in *Flamingo Narcissus, Como Zoo, Saint Paul, Minnesota*, offers another lesson in assessing visual weight. A mirror image of the flamingo is reflected in the water as she drinks. The bird and her reflection are of roughly equal size, but the reflection is darker, appears in the lower-third of the frame, is disrupted by the ripples in the water, and is lower in contrast and saturation. The bird itself is featured in

▼ *The Kid Stays in the Picture, Lowry Bridge, Minneapolis*

Flamingo Narcissus, Como Zoo, Saint Paul, Minnesota ▶

the top two-thirds of the frame (where the Western eye is trained to begin reading, from left to right). While darker objects tend to be perceived as having more visual weight (look at how the black tip of the bird's bill draws the eye), the reflection of the bird is harder to see clearly, and so the eye slips over it and returns to the bright pink feathers of the bird's body.

There are numerous leading lines in the photo—so many that they almost disrupt each other (especially the ripples in the water). The flamingo's neck forms the clearest and strongest line, however, and most of it rests against the strong, contrasting green background. The bird's head, which is a lighter pink, has a broken background, alternating green with bright white; where the head abuts the white water, the strength of the grounding weakens, and there is lower contrast. The zig-zag of the flamingo's neck activates the viewer's eyes to follow the line to the bird's head, where the white eye is in just enough contrast to the darker facial feathers to "land" the viewer's gaze on the flamingo's face. The black beak terminates the gaze by being the darkest element in the frame (almost like a period at the end of a sentence). The bird's reflection simply isn't strong enough to counter-balance the strong visual cues of the bird itself or to engage the viewer in gazing at the reflection as intently.

Lighting

Lighting describes the sources of illumination that are detected by a camera sensor and recorded in a file or on a piece of film. In photo analysis, lighting is considered in terms of how it exposes the subject. A photograph can be interrogated for whether the photographer used available light, studio light, or light that was otherwise manipulated. Lighting choices invoke culturally agreed-upon ideas about mood, veracity, and the importance of an element in a frame.

Natural lighting is often a feature of photojournalism: there is a belief that a photo taken in natural lighting records an event faithfully, without manipulation. Sometimes a "natural" look is boosted by the use of flash. Studio lighting is often used to heighten effects in a dramatic style. Studio lights can be moved and altered in their intensity to emphasize some aspects of what's in the frame and to play down or hide others. A photographer can make choices about when and where to shoot a photograph in natural light, and how to set exposure in the camera, and these can also heighten effects in the same way that studio lighting does. Viewers tend to believe that some styles of shooting are less manipulative or premeditated than others, and we grant more authenticity to these. Sometimes this naturalistic style is referred to as "straight photography."

Early debates about the nature of photography centered on whether the recording of light onto film was science or art. One perspective held that photography was more objective, accurate, and thorough than human description or accounting because a machine did the recording (even though a human directed the machine). Another perspective looked on cameras

14

▲ *Delphinium Blues*

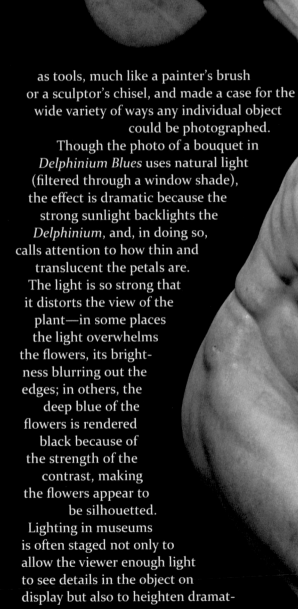

as tools, much like a painter's brush or a sculptor's chisel, and made a case for the wide variety of ways any individual object could be photographed.

Though the photo of a bouquet in *Delphinium Blues* uses natural light (filtered through a window shade), the effect is dramatic because the strong sunlight backlights the *Delphinium*, and, in doing so, calls attention to how thin and translucent the petals are. The light is so strong that it distorts the view of the plant—in some places the light overwhelms the flowers, its brightness blurring out the edges; in others, the deep blue of the flowers is rendered black because of the strength of the contrast, making the flowers appear to be silhouetted.

Lighting in museums is often staged not only to allow the viewer enough light to see details in the object on display but also to heighten dramat-ic effects. The key lighting on the statue of a Discobolus (*Discus Thrower*) is directed from the top and to the side to emphasize the hyper-realistic qualities of musculature and veins.

With more ordinary, flat lighting (say, to fully light the face), the statue would look quite different, and a viewer might miss the skill the sculptor put into capturing the moment when the momentum of preparing to throw the discus caused the figure to pivot.

Diffused Lighting

The Thinker: St. Paul ▲

In a low-contrast lighting situation, the viewer is required to discern subtle gradations of tonal range. In *The Thinker: St. Paul*, the subject was in a dimly-lit room, and most of the available light was filtered through a window and diffused so broadly through the room that the shadows were only strong in the box with the man. While the photo has a strong black register to anchor the subject's visual weight, he is, overall, a series of shades of gray. Note how the marble cap around his box, though sharply in focus, almost blends into the marble floor behind it. The subject's face is slightly brighter than the fist he is resting it on, but it still seems muted in this scene. With low lighting, a photographer runs the risk of creating a shadowy or dull composition, and low light can make sharp focus difficult (especially without a tripod). One may hope for a moody result, as here, but runs the risk of a bland one. In this photo, I was aiming to show a person mired in his surroundings, boxed in and disaffected. Rendering the subject in a series of grays with a gray palette around him and a black palette below was meant to emphasize this mired feeling. More dynamic contrast in the lighting would have added unwanted energy to the scene.

Diffused lighting is also referred to as "ambient lighting," which means that the light uniformly covers everything that is in the frame, decreasing the impact of any one-directional light that might be present. The image of a cornice and corbel (the horizontal molding and the stone bracket that helps support it) of a medieval cathedral in *Naughty Acrobat in Cahors, France*, taken in the shadow of another, taller building, has an even, ambient lighting. Though some shadow can be seen on the underside of the projection, there isn't a clear sense of where the light in the scene is coming from, except that it is slightly brighter coming in from the left foreground. Because the sculpture's face is turned to the left and towards the viewer, that slight boost in lighting in front (along with a slight shadow for the side of his head) makes his face "pop" as the most compelling part of the photo.

▲ *Naughty Acrobat in Cahors, France*

Key Lighting

Key lighting usually refers to single-point, artificial brightness pointed at a strategic part of the subject. It can also be seen, in its strongest forms, as a spotlight. Key lighting is often used in films to bathe a subject in light, differentiating him/her/it from shadowy surroundings. In all of photography, it can be used with more or less emphasis and doesn't have to be an artificial light.

With the glass decanter and sphere in *Crystal Ball and Antique Decanter*, I used strong sunlight from a window behind the set-up as my only lighting, keeping the source one-directional in an otherwise dark room. The light through the window created high contrast between the surfaces that it hit directly and those too far away for light to register on the camera's sensor. A black backdrop was placed behind the decanter, which allowed a patch of darkness to develop at the upper-center of the bottle.

The key light draws the eye to the crenellated rim of the decanter and to the point at which the light is most strongly concentrated in the ball in the foreground. The high contrast renders the background a velvety black surrounding the brightly-lit subject. The green drape the ball rests on is picked up and inverted, in the top of the sphere, creating a strong green silhouette. Because the sphere inverts the light passing through it, the bright key light from window above is shown in the base of the ball.

▲ *Crystal Ball and Antique Decanter*
The Wine Comes Highly Recommended (Ravenna, Italy) ▶

Key lighting can happen within the frame of a photo even when there are other competing light sources. In *The Wine Comes Highly Recommended (Ravenna, Italy)*, a sun-ray from a very high, small window appears as a shaft of light, and lands on the wine glass. The camera caught it at that moment, before it moved to the customer and caused him to change his position. The restaurant was fairly dark, but diffused light came from windows closer to the ground. You can see that the customer is also backlit by another window behind him, which was cropped out of the frame. The effect of the key light was to make the glass of wine, otherwise rather unremarkable in the frame, seem as though it was the most significant thing in the photo. In this image, the light was a fortuitous accident, but studio photographers in particular use key lighting in just this way to direct an audience's attention within a busy image.

Backlight

When a key light (or even a larger light source) catches the subject from behind, it is called a rim light because it creates a kind of halo effect. Backlight can create a silhouette effect if the light in front of the subject is too weak to compete with the light source behind it. The sculpture in *Pegasus in Bomarzo* has enough light in front for you to see the details of the Pegasus, and the background light is not so strong that it obliterates the trees. The difference between the two, however, is strong enough to heighten the drama of the shot.

Pegasus in Bomarzo ▶

▼ *Herons on the Mississippi River*

When backlight hits something gauzy or translucent, that element may appear to be a light source in its own right. In *Charlotte Has Nothing to Say*, the spider and web, in front of a window that I cropped out of the frame, are so brightly lit that they both glow. Only the spider's abdomen is thick enough to show up as a shadow. The light coming from the crack between the window and the sill is so strong that it renders the details of the web invisible where they intersect. In this example, the silhouette effect, expected when a subject is strongly back-lit, is inverted because the subject itself is barely substantive enough to stand up to the light source.

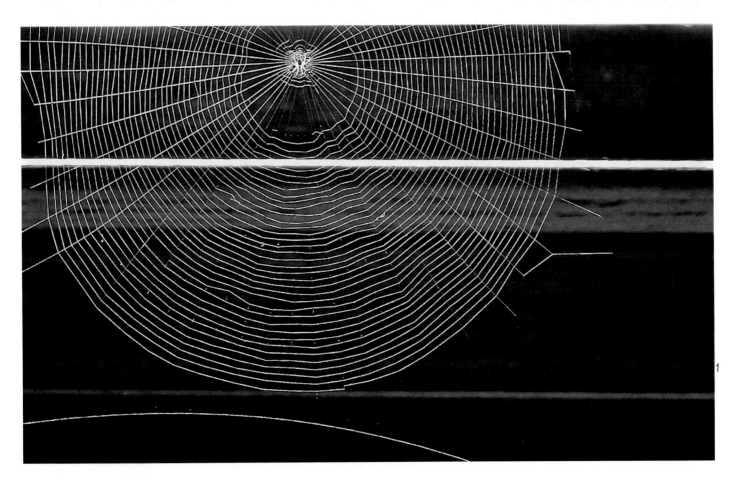

Charlotte Has Nothing to Say ▲

Flat Light

On a very cloudy day, the sky can be bright, but the light will seem to be coming from all directions or none in particular. This is good light for portraiture (because your subject won't be squinting into the sun or overshadowed by bright light coming from behind), but it can also take dimensionality and detail out of a photo. In *Herons on the Mississippi River*, for instance, the sky seems like a plain backdrop. The contrast between the blue heron and the sky is strong but looks jarring: the bird seems isolated from any context as it might in a painting of the bird alone with no other depth of field. Because the light is fairly even, the heron's front is not in shadow even though the backlight is so strong. There are lots of details here, but the bird, although in focus and strongly lit, seems washed out. Flat light (usually bright and diffused) can seem almost "clinical" and tends to produce a sterile image, draining energy from a scene. Even though this bird is in a dramatic mid-flight moment, the light quality makes him appear more suspended than in action.

Flat light is very good for documenting flat subjects in which you want to see all aspects with the same level of clarity and detail. The fifth-century mosaic in *Christ Mosaic in Ravenna, Italy* is lit evenly, and has no obvious shadows, even though the surface of the mosaic is concave. Such a photo is suitable for academic or museum use.

▲ *Christ Mosaic in Ravenna, Italy*
Duomo, Orvieto ▶

Hard Light

Hard light (*Duomo, Orvieto*) is often experienced as full sunlight. It is very bright, can almost overwhelm its subject, and usually produces harsh shadows that block part of a scene. Hard light is often used in post-cards, which aim to show a subject as vividly as possible, with a sensibility that brightness and sharpness are exciting. Hard light can yield beautiful photographs, but many photographers feel that the even, bright light is not as interesting as the slanted light of early morning or late afternoon (which they refer to as "the golden hour"—when light is yellower and is diffused through the moisture and particulates in the air between the viewer and the horizon).

Tonal Range and Contrast

A discussion of lighting in photography addresses how intensity and gradations of light and color (where appropriate) appear in a frame. Perception of tonal range can vary based on the capacity of a camera's sensor, a printer, or a computer screen. Whatever the end product, the viewer will react to the strength of the differences between lightness and darkness, diffusion and concentration of color and light.

Photographers use these elements to affect mood in a photo and to direct a viewer to where they want emphasis in the subject. Tonal range refers to the spectrum of color (or, sometimes, the spectrum within a certain color, such as from a yellow-green to a blue-green). Dynamic range can refer to the relative brightness or darkness in a frame (from a bright white to a shadow so dark no detail is discernible). A tonal range can be discussed in terms of lightness to darkness (baby blue to navy), and it can be discussed in terms of its intensity (flat blue paint to a neon blue light or "day-glow"). Contrast is the sharpness of differences within a frame (gradations of light or color versus startling jumps to ends of the spectrum with little in between).

24

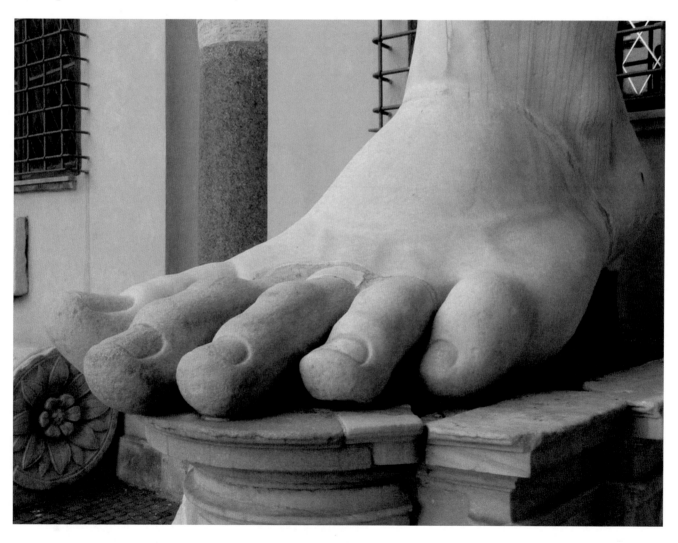

The tonal range in *Constantine's Toes* is not very broad. Because of the diffused light, the scene is mostly shades of light-gold-to-beige. There is enough contrast in the frame to create a true black and a true white, but those extremes are overwhelmed by the yellowy palette. The small amount of white lattice work in the upper-right corner is the only point of striking contrast in the frame—it almost seems to leap out of the picture when compared to the rest of the elements. The dynamic range of this photo is quite broad, as is its tonal range.

Emperor of Butterflies ▲
◀ *Constantine's Toes*

The butterfly in *Emperor of Butterflies* is a vivid orange-red nearest its body, while the greenery in the photo is a strong, bright, yellow-green. The white elements in the wing show up strongly, especially where they are close to the black border elements. Where the wings shadow the butterfly's body, the black and white aren't as strong in contrast and intensity. The forelegs don't stand out in strong contrast to the wings or the leaf they grasp—not just because they are in shadow, but because the brown isn't that far in the tonal range from the green or the darker orange of the wings. The tonal range of the leaves is not broad, but it is noticeable: the sunlit green is more intense and yellow in the sunlight, and the out-of-focus greenery tends to be less vivid where it is in shadow.

The architects of the building in *Art Deco in Saint Paul* set out to create a very dramatic scene. The gold elements and the black ones stand in strong contrast to each other: the gold is a saturated color, and the black marble is its more matte and light-absorbing foil. The monumental sculpture is white but bathed in golden light. It is the strength of the light as it hits the abdomen of the statue that provides the brightest point in the photo. The mirrored ceiling multiplies the light and adds to the drama, but you'll notice, even though the mirror reflects the statue, that its distance from the statue renders the light dimmer and yellower. The tonal range of the yellows in this image is not very broad, and the black range is almost uniform throughout. The effect is unreal and intentionally overwhelming to the viewer, who is dwarfed and literally over-shadowed by the lighting arrangement. The head of the statue is the focal point of the scene, not just because of the single-point perspective, but because the level of highest dynamic contrast is between its key-lit head and the black, recessed alcove behind it.

Perspective

The word "perspective" can be used in two different senses as we analyze photos. The first is its generic sense, equivalent to the term "point of view." When used this way, the perspective of the photo may be termed as the perceived viewpoint of the photographer as a witness to the scene. In *Portrait of the Artist, New Orleans*, for example, I wanted to create a portrait of an artist, and, because he is a sculptor, I chose to focus on his hands. The perspective I took with my camera was to lower the lens to the subject's chest-level and stand close enough to him that his body filled the frame. This perspective (point of view) stands out because it is not at an adult's eye-level and thereby compels the viewer to interpret the subject without his face, which is usually the key identifier of a person in a portrait. What a viewer might not know, without a caption, is that the pendant on the subject's chest is a two-dimensional representation of one of his more famous works of art. Thus, in the frame is the artist as portrayed by

▲ *Art Deco in Saint Paul*
Portrait of the Artist, New Orleans ▶

an image of his work and his hands—the means by which he made the sculpture. A positioning of the camera that is noticeably different from how viewers would regard a subject with their own eyes in real life is said to have a distinctive perspective.

In the geometric/artistic sense of perspective, one has to specify particular kinds. Many photographs have single-point perspective, where the depth of field in the photo causes the eye to travel to a vanishing point that seems to go deepest into the scene.

Single-Point Perspective

An image like *Nave of Santa Maria in Trastevere* uses single-point perspective to explain how the construction of early churches (in this case, a fifth-century church in Rome) used perspective to focus the attention of attendees to services. A dizzying array of surfaces and decorative elements play out on the walls and ceiling, explaining key themes of the religion and recounting diverse stories. The attention is nonetheless focused as one enters the building: the patterned floor draws the eye to the altar, which is framed by the archway that contains the apse.

Note that the altar itself is slightly raised and contains an image of Christ, making the image the literal focal point of all

28

the rituals that transpire there. In the photograph, single-point perspective is reinforced by the distortion in the image: the parallel lines of the floor appear to converge as they travel from the lower-edge of the frame up to near-center. The archways telescope down into a smaller focal area. The ciborium (the structure built over the altar) frames the altar as a center point. Most of the lines in the photo point toward the central part of the image. There are few distractions to turn the eye anywhere else and, when one element does distract (such as the man in the right pew facing toward the outside of the frame), it seems jarring.

A single-point perspective shouldn't be confused with merely identifying the center of the photo. In the image *Cathedral*, we see a macrophotograph of a dahlia. The leading lines in the image all point to the right-hand third of the photo, where the center of the flower is. The photo is a flat surface, but the radiating petals of the flower, which are of increasing sizes the farther they are from the center, create a sense of depth. Because the frame is filled by the flower, the rhythm of all the petals converging on the center of the flower creates a single-point perspective based on the midpoint of the flower and not of the photo.

◀ *Nave of Santa Maria in Trastevere*
Cathedral ▶

Two-Point Perspective

Two-point perspective is less common and takes some concentration to perceive. While the shadows of the trees point toward the entryway of the bakery in *Lake Street Panaderia San Miguel (Minneapolis),* the building is at an intersection, with its front-facing corner squared-off. The eye is taken in two different directions: to the left and to the right. The left view is blocked a bit by the tree, but the right view veers off at an angle and leads out of the frame. The way that the building juts forward at the corner blunts the possibility that the center of the frame will have a single vanishing point. The depth of the image is shown on opposite edges of the frame.

Three-Point Perspective

Three-point perspective is still more subtle. Where two-point perspective is often seen on the horizontal axis in a photo, the third point of perspective introduces the vertical access in a more pronounced way.

Dome of the Minnesota State Capitol is very complicated in its perspectives. On the one hand, you can see the stairs in the

Lake Street Panaderia San Miguel (Minneapolis) ▼

▲ *Dome of the Minnesota State Capitol*

distance as a single-vanishing point, but the other elements in the composition somewhat sabotage this orienta-tion. The black ovals in the foreground lead the eye outside of the frame and into two oppositional arcs. The balus-trade that surrounds the opening in the floor takes the viewer's eye downward into the gallery below. The points in the star that is a mosaic on the ground floor encourage the eye to vector off in multiple directions, and the small-er star contained in the mosaic acts as its own illusory vanishing point. The overall effect is rather disorienting because the image explores depth of field vertically and horizontally, without creating a definitive point of focus.

Planar Perspective

There are other, even more dizzying forms of perspective, but the last example I want to discuss is perhaps the most useful for analyzing photos: planar perspective. Essentially, this can be thought of as all the perceived surfaces in an image which can be used to introduce the idea of depth, often signaled by the comparative sizes of recognizable objects suggesting distance between those objects. The most common planes of a realistic photo (one in which the objects seem recognizable from real life) are described as foreground, middle ground, and background.

The first pass at describing the composition of *Cane Boiling Cauldron, Whitney Plantation, Louisiana* is easy: the broken cauldron for cane sugar production is in the foreground, and a lawn stretches between the cauldron and the slave cabins. The lawn can be termed the middle ground or plane.

The slave cabins are the background. In reality, the elements in the frame are all at the same distance from the viewer: it's a flat surface. However, the broken cauldron is in the lower third of the frame and is larger than anything else in the frame. The grass, a thin strip running unbroken across the middle of the frame, is so featureless that it reads as negative space. The cabins are in the upper-middle of the photo, and we interpret them as farther away because they are smaller than the cauldron; in real life, we understand that houses are bigger than cauldrons, and so we attribute depth to the image to preserve that understanding.

Senate Chamber, Minnesota State Capitol ▲
◀ *Cane Boiling Cauldron, Whitney Plantation, Louisiana*

33

Technically, the sky is the back-most plane in the image—it is in the upper third of the photo and forms an almost blank ground for the figure that is the cabin. In the same way, the brighter grass is a ground for the darker figure of the cauldron. The cauldron's scale and contrasting darkness give it the most visual weight in the frame, even though all the elements register as fairly consistently in focus. Even though the shot is distorted by the wide-angle lens, the multi-planar perspective conveys depth and creates an air of realism.

In *Senate Chamber, Minnesota State Capitol*, a view of a ceiling in the Minnesota State Capitol, the image looks up at a dome with five slices cut into it at several angles. At the bottom of the photo, an arch forms a visual base. This arch curves above a tympanum and seems to support a central skylight (enclosed in a horseshoe arch) that serves as one vanishing point in the photo's perspective. This skylight is at the top of the dome, on a plane more distant from the viewer.

34

The five concave slices show arches outlined in white that "lean in" at different angles, directing the eye both toward and away from the central skylight. The points of these arches lead the eye towards the center skylight high above. Inside each white arch is a green arch suggesting yet another plane just a bit higher above the viewer than the white arches. As they radiate around the skylight, each of these white or green arches appears to be a planar surface tipped at a different angle towards the horseshoe arch and skylight. At the same time, the eye is also directed away from the central skylight by the four upper "arms" of the six-pointed star implied by all the cut-outs in the dome. These arms form planes in their own right, because they appear closer to the viewer than the dark recesses inside the white arches. Each of these "arm" planes suggests a finger pointing away from the center skylight. Still other planes and directions for eye travel are suggested by the gold colored arches (with multiple lights in them) that radiate around the edges of the photo. I lost count after twenty of all the surfaces that assert themselves as distinct from others in the photo. The effect is disorienting. Nonetheless, the image conveys a very believable sense of a 3D object, even though the photo stubbornly remains two-dimensional.

▲ *Civita di Bagnoregio*
On the Levee ▶

Atmospheric or Aerial Perspective

This type of perspective takes into account how particles or humidity in the air, viewed from a distance, change how we perceive objects that are far from us. When I show you this photo of a hilltop town (*Civita di Bagnoregio*), I can assure you that the hills in the background have the same geologic and botanic makeup as the hill in the foreground, but you'll note that they are of a different color and are less in contrast than the hill that is the subject of the image. The farther away that objects appear to us, up to and including the horizon line, the more they become bluer or grayer, and their details fade. The saturation of the farther element decreases and blends with the background. Photographers can use this visual technique to create a dreamy effect. In *On the Levee*, the bird on the pier is in sharp focus and silhouette, but the shore behind it seems cloudy, with a narrower tonal range. If we were standing on the opposite shore, we'd experience the environment around us as sharper in all details of color and brightness, and the bird on the pier would be harder to discern. Atmospheric perspective in a photo creates a sense of

depth. Because objects in the distance lose their sharpness and saturation, we assume they are farther away. In *Highlights of Paris, France*, an image that was processed to be highly contrasting in the first place, the viewer still notices that the Eiffel Tower is farther away than the Ferris wheel, the monumental statue, and the obelisk. The Tower is less solid and more detailed than the statue and the obelisk, but, because it is farther away, it appears gray instead of true black.

◀ *Eye of the Peacock*

Curvilinear Perspective

This type of perspective is not often seen in photography or art but is usually striking because the surreal effect of representing a bending surface creates multiple vanishing points. In real-world viewing, our vision doesn't typically entertain multiple vanishing points, but rather focuses us on one at a time. A photo allows us to look at something all at once in a way our normal vision won't.

In *Eye of the Peacock*, I placed a clear glass sphere in front of a peacock feather. The ball inverts and bends the image of the feather. Because the feather in the shot is framed behind the glass ball, the viewer can see a flatter image as the bokeh, while the distorted image is in focus, creating a sort of visual paradox.

Camera Angle

The direction and proximity of the camera lens to the subject can greatly affect a viewer's perspective. A camera is "angled" by tipping it toward or away from the subject within a range of about 120 degrees vertically (handheld or with a tripod), getting closer or farther away from the subject (or using a lens to zoom in or out), or moving the camera horizontally somewhere within a 180-degree range of the subject. Certain camera angles have become traditional for communicating particular sentiments or attitudes.

◀ *Highlights of Paris, France*

Close-Up

Getting near enough to a human subject that the body or face fills the frame is termed a "close-up" shot. This can also work with inanimate objects. Typically, this angle suggests intimacy and becomes more powerful when the subject/object is recognizable and viewers can recognize they are seeing part of a whole. In a shot like *Endymion*, a feeling of voyeurism or intimacy is generated because the camera puts the viewer a lot closer to an unaware person than would be customarily acceptable. A close-up gives the viewer a chance to view a subject in great detail and at leisure, whereas taboos about staring and invading personal space exist in real life.

39

Hanging by His Mittens ▲
◄ *Endymion*

An extreme close-up may bring viewers closer than they want to be to the subject and can read as a demand to look more actively. As *Hanging by His Mittens* shows, an extreme close-up may frame the subject only partially, but in sharp detail, as is common in macro-photography.

High Angle

Shooting a subject from above can diminish the subject, making it seem either cute or less significant. The viewer takes on the perspective of the camera and can thereby feel superior to or metaphorically "above" the subject. For this reason, photographers of children and pets are frequently disposed to shoot at the subjects' own eye-level or from below—if adults usually experience a child or pet from a high-angle view, the surprise and intimacy of a lower angle creates more emotional impact. Food photography uses high angles in order to get a complete view of the dish, and landscape photography employs high angles sometimes to give one a sense of the vastness of a place, while at the same time lending the audience an "eagle's eye" or "bird's eye" view. The sense of distance from the subject can make a viewer more comfortable or detached.

In *Torretta Pepoli, Erice, Sicily*, the crumbling castle is shot from a much higher cliff, and the scale of the castle is diminished because it is viewed alongside a cliff face that has greater scale than it does. If the camera were right next to the castle, the structure would loom above the human scale and seem more impressive.

40

Low Angle

Placing the camera below a subject makes it seem more remote or imposing. The statue of *Nike of Samothrace, Louvre Museum, Paris* is in itself about life-size on human scale, but the museum has placed the statue on a stand that is like the prow of a large ship and situated it on the upper landing of a grand staircase, which gives the statue visual weight and a majestic stance. Shooting the subject from a low angle increases the drama intrinsic to the statue's flowing drapery and spread wings.

41

In architectural photography, one often faces a building from the ground and points the camera upward to take in the whole structure. When the camera sensor is tilted up, the bottom of the building is read as closer and wider, and the top of the building appears to recede at an angle. This phenomenon is known as "keystoning."

Nike of Samothrace, Louvre Museum, Paris ▲
◄ *Torretta Pepoli, Erice, Sicily*

In *Capitol and Quadriga, Saint Paul, Minnesota*, a shot of the dome of the Minnesota State Capitol, the building's roof appears to slope away rather than to face the viewer fully upright. The narrowing of the building as it ends in its roof lantern at the top contributes to this illusion by making the dome appear triangular or arrow-shaped against the ground of the sky rather than square with a hemispherical top. The human eye usually corrects this point of view when looking up, so it can be a surprise when a building in a photograph looks distorted compared to the way it appeared in person. Photographers can use tilt-shift lenses or post-production software to correct unwanted slanting.

Ready for His Close-Up, Lucca, Italy ▶

▼ *Capitol and Quadriga, Saint Paul, Minnesota*

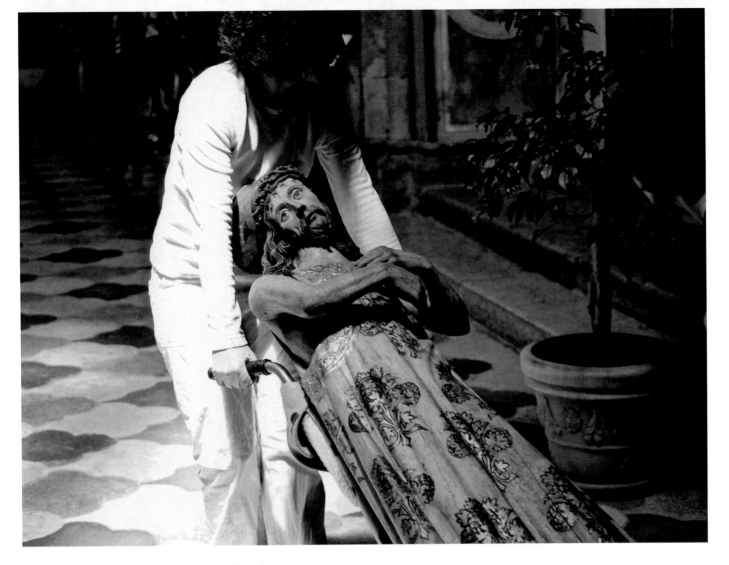

Medium Shot/Eye-Level Angle

A "medium shot" is a term borrowed from cinematography and describes when the camera renders the subject at the same level as the average human perspective. This can also be termed "eye-level" because the angle endeavors to make the viewer feel roughly parallel to the subject. The mood that this camera angle can create is to give the viewer the impression of being in the middle of the scene itself, and that's one reason the medium shot is very popular in street photography (and, in fact, almost defines it). *Ready for His Close-Up, Lucca, Italy*, shows an art preservationist removing a statue for retouching. The preservationist, in white, is at roughly the same scale as I was when I encountered her, and the medium shot is reinforced by the fact that the statue itself is life-sized and life-like and seems to gaze directly into the camera. Photojournalism uses this angle for a similar kind of shock value—the viewer is given the sense that she encounters something usually remote and unapproachable as on the same level.

Side Angle

Positioning the camera off-center from a subject can lend it more volume and a sense of movement. A photo is a flat surface, and Westerners are taught to read a page-like form from left to right; in looking at a photo, the eye sweeps the frame to take it all in, and a subject not shown in full-frontal stance may be perceived as more dynamic because of that motion of the eye, seeing something that is turned from it.

If I had stood directly in front of the ancient Greek temple in *Temple of Concord, Agrigento, Sicily*, the resulting image would have seemed quite flat and static. The positioning of the camera to the right of and below the building gave depth to the subject.

The abandoned chairs in *Wall Flowers* were lined up against a fence. Photographing them at an angle perpendicular to the fence would have flattened them out. The side-angle, and the fortuitous lurch of the right-hand chair, gives the scene a sense of passing time and progressing decay because the chairs seem to lean or tumble toward the viewer.

◀ *Temple of Concord, Agrigento, Sicily*

Wall Flowers ▼

Long Shot

In a long shot, the subject is usually extremely small and positioned in the background of the photo. The camera angle is used to express insignificance or the sense that something small is about to come into closer, sharper focus. This can be ominous or hopeful. A long shot is not so much a matter of angle of the camera as a decision about framing and depth of field. It is difficult to make the smallest thing in your frame the focal point because there is the risk of losing the visual weight that is required to catch the viewer's attention. In such instances, photographers may rely on a strong figure-to-ground contrast to call attention to the figure (as you'll notice in *Canada Geese, Minneapolis, Minnesota*, in the Nature Photography section.)

The subject in *The Worm's Head, Rhosilli, Wales*, is a tourist location, a tidal island accessible by foot at low tide. This landscape shot was framed to emphasize the way the island points out to sea, as a far-away, almost illusory place. To convey this, I walked to where the head (the right-most outcropping of rock) would be angled away from the viewer, to seem as though the "worm" (a medieval term for "dragon" or "serpent") was swimming away. The countryside leading to the worm occupies the middle- and

The Worm's Head, Rhosilli, Wales ▼

46

foreground, with the hiking path acting as a leading line to the tail of the worm. While the cliffs in the middle-ground loom larger and are clearer because of aerial perspective, the leading lines extend the long shot to the background of the picture where the Worm's Head lies.

Wide camera angles are dealt with at length in the "Distortion" section of this book.

Genre

Specific types of photography are grouped into categories, based on their subjects, their subject matter, and their style. When you know the genre of photography to which an image belongs, you can understand what the focus of the image is, the artistic tradition that produced it, the conventions regarding how such an image should be shot, and the types of equipment that are common to that photographic category. Next, I will give you a brief definition (and, in most cases, an example) of the genre.

Landscape Photography

This genre of photography is given to panoramic vistas of territory, often without urban areas featured. Landscape photographers often employ natural lighting and use wide-angle lenses, which can introduce distortion into their shots; they may use tilt-shift lenses, anti-keystoning software in their cameras, or corrective functions in their post-production software as ways to make their images seem

▲ *Sydney Sunrise*

realistic—or, at least, not distracting to the viewer. Amateur photographers may use the automated "landscape" function on their cameras, which contains algorithms to heighten whites, greens, and blues (typical colors found in landscapes), and create greater depth of field by using a control on the aperture for high f-stop numbers.

Landscape photographers often evoke a sense of awe by framing subjects to emphasize their monumental scale. A seascape can also be a landscape photo. In *Sydney Sunrise*, the stark contrast between the orange sky, the dark clouds, and the even darker ocean create a striping effect that makes this image seem almost like an abstract minimalist painting. It's an unaltered, hand-held shot of a sunrise, but the monumental scale of the objects in the frame lend it a more dramatic and stagey aspect.

Nature Photography

While landscape photography seems identical to nature photography, this genre in fact encompasses more than the landscape. Because of that, its range of techniques is also broader. Nature photography may focus on smaller scenes than a wide landscape and on smaller subjects (a stand of trees, or animals, birds, plants, or insects, e.g.). Floral photography may fall within the category of nature photography, but, if the flowers are brought into a studio environment, the photos are usually categorized as fine-art photography.

Nature photographers may use telephoto lenses for wildlife because the long range of a telephoto lens allows them to photograph subjects without startling them or disturbing their habitats. These photographers may employ high shutter speeds or use flash, especially at night, to capture a darkened subject as well as to freeze action (a flash will fire for a fraction of a second and can be timed to the shutter speed). *Canada Geese, Minneapolis, Minnesota* required a telephoto lens and a tripod. The geese were on an island, a protected habitat in the middle of a river, so they were able to move around without concern for the spectators on the opposite shore. Note that the sand acts as a good figure-to-ground framing device for both birds.

Nature photographers who focus on plants, small animals, and insects may use macro lenses to bring out details in tiny subjects. Macro lenses have very wide apertures, resulting in a shallow depth-of-field. This

Dying Hosta ▶

▼ *Canada Geese, Minneapolis, Minnesota*

allows a lot of light to enter the lens for a faster exposure, but it also means that only a sliver of the subject might be in focus (such as the pistil and stamen of a flower, but not its petals), with much of the subject rendered as bokeh. Macro photographers might use tripods and flash to enable a longer exposure and deeper depth of field; some use ring-flash units, a circle of lighting meant to fit around the lens of the camera, to ensure targeted, intense light release. Macrophotographers may carry small circular reflectors in white or gold to boost the ambient light around their subjects, without the reflector appearing in the frame (video, portrait, and fashion photography employ reflectors like these, only larger). The macro-shooting mode setting on a camera will ensure an exposure with a wide aperture and perhaps also trigger an automated flash.

The super-sharp quality of the macro lens used in *Dying Hosta* allows the viewer to see these dying *Hosta* leaves at a greater than 1:1 ratio. The effect of this is to invite viewers into a world more detailed than they might notice if they observed the plant in real life.

Night Photography/Astrophotography

Night photography, like most macrophotography, tends to use wide-aperture lenses to take in a dim subject (such as stars in the sky). Night photography usually relies on long shutter releases (one second to more than a minute) to gather light, however. Urban night photography may have enough ambient street light to permit shorter exposures, but a tripod, which keeps the camera still while it takes that long exposure, is standard equipment in much night photography. The average person can hold a camera still for about a 1/60 of a second, though newer, high-end cameras with complex image-stabilization mechanics have been pushing that boundary closer to one second.

In night photography of non-astral subjects, darkness is used to create a surreal, dramatic, or gritty mood. Astrophotography can range from an amateur with a tripod setting up a two- to four-second exposure for photographing the moon (with an exposure longer than that, the movement of the moon will blur the image), to a scientist using a camera attached to a high-powered telescope. (In the most sophisticated astrophotography

settings, the sponsoring organization may have worked with the local government to switch street lights off synchronously for unnoticeable—to the human eye—fractions of a second so that the telescope cameras can shoot with less light pollution).

In this night scene, *La Crêpe Nanou, New Orleans, Louisiana*, I used the bright available light emanating from the street lamps and the restaurant itself to illuminate the scene, making a handheld shot feasible. The darkness of the night sky in the top-third of the frame, and the bright reflection of light off the sidewalk in the bottom third, create an interesting contrast of grounds to the figure of the restaurant.

Solar Eclipse 2017 required me to use a dark filter over the telephoto lens of my camera (set on a tripod) to protect the equipment and my eyes from the intense brightness, but also to make a defined exposure possible. (The filter took the near-impossibly brief shutter speed for this image down to something slow enough to render some detail in the shot. While the filter gave the image this orange-and-black color, I didn't alter it to something more natural-looking because I liked the dramatic effect.)

Solar Eclipse 2017 ▲

◀ *La Crêpe Nanou, New Orleans, Louisiana*

Street Photography

The name of this genre may seem self-descriptive, but professionals in this category of photography have been developing conventions and codes of ethics to regulate their practice. In street photography, there is an attitude of witnessing social life as it happens, emphasizing the interplay of human scale with the larger scale of the abstracted geometry of buildings, pavement, and other structures (like cars or lamp posts or garbage cans).

The street scene in *Walking in Perugia*, taken on an Italian street, was my endeavor to capture modern people in the context of their ancient cityscape. The building's scale dwarfs them, and they recede as they walk down the hill from the viewer. The contrasting darkness of the street in shadow makes the old walls and archways seem mysterious, and the stairs lead above the walkers into darkness.

Street photography tends to employ lenses that maintain a perspective consistent with human vision (35- or 50-millimeter lenses are popular because they are close to the viewpoint of the human eye in angle-range of view and depth of focus). Exposures can be short, to catch a decisive moment by freezing action, or long, to blur moving figures and convey the constant motion of the average street scene.

▲ *Walking in Perugia*
The Saint of Cocullo ▶

Many street photographers like to be as inconspicuous as possible so they can capture people without their awareness in what are termed "candid shots." To support this unobtrusiveness, street photographers rarely carry lots of extra equipment such as tripods, big lights, or reflectors. Professionals who want to profit from their photographs will carry model-release forms so they can ask individuals who are identifiable in their shots to give permission for the photos to be published and to give up any rights to proceeds from the sale of the images. There are, however, laws in most states which abrogate an individual's right to privacy in a public domain, allowing street photographers more leeway in the use of photos of subjects in public.

The subject in *The Saint of Cocullo*, photographed while he was carrying a cross in a religious procession, was clearly having a much more intimate and serious experience than the spectators watching him. My own place in the crowd, with a 150mm-equivalent lens, allowed me to get closer to him than would otherwise have been possible or polite and to isolate his experience from the crowd of photographers who were focused on other parts of the parade.

Photojournalism

Photojournalism may employ many of the techniques of street photography. The intention is often to capture an event's meaning on a human scale and to make viewers feel they are almost present to witness the event. Therefore, 35- to 50mm lenses are often employed. Where events involve crowds, however, a telephoto lens takes advantage of the option to isolate individual actors from a crowd. A wide-angle lens might also be used to capture a massive event or to give the audience a perspective on an event that literally calls on them to see "the big picture." Photojournalists, like street photographers, may travel light on equipment, so that their presence doesn't alter the behavior of subjects who know they're being filmed. Shooting vulnerable individuals is a continual concern for professional photojournalists because the potential for exploiting or aestheticizing the suffering of others is great.

An important difference between street photography and photojournalism is that photojournalists must be rigorous not to distort or alter photos for artistic effect. Photos in news journals are expected to be representations of truth, and alteration is therefore looked upon as deception.

Photojournalists may, however, seek ways to create metaphoric or metonymic images in order to convey an idea they don't want to use human subjects to express. Photographing damaged toys in the rubble of a bombed building, instead

of photographing injured children, might be one example.

In *It Was Here*, I wanted to capture the tragedy of the ruined lives in the aftermath of Hurricane Katrina in the Lower Ninth Ward of New Orleans without subjecting any of the remaining residents to my intrusion. I chose this destroyed house, graffitied with a statement by one of the residents, to express the loss of life and community and the resultant, enduring pain.

Travel Photography

While this genre, as with photojournalism, seeks to inform viewers about actual places, it has much more license to be artistic and creative because it is often used to encourage the viewer to travel and can be sponsored by businesses that stand to benefit from tourism.

◀ *It Was Here*   *Saint Vader* ▶

Travel photography tries to walk a line between being familiarly iconic (that is, invoking some visual aspect the viewer already knows about a place) and being enticingly surprising (spurring the desire for exploration/adventure in the viewer). Although there are voyeuristic photographers who advertise for what's termed "disaster tourism," most travel photographers want to keep things light and fun, and so they may emphasize bright colors and romantic, misty views of their subjects. People may be featured in travel photography, but they're usually framed as types, rather than individuals. They can be depicted as "local color," meaning they are unusual and exotic to the intended audience, and an example of how fun or interesting a place can be; in such a case, they are models representing a place, not individuals in portraiture.

The street performer in *Saint Vader*, photographed in the French Quarter of New Orleans, performed a dance to a musical show he'd enhanced with sound and light equipment, and he was there to be noticed and tipped. His Darth Vader costume riffed on the city's passion for its football team, the New Orleans Saints. In the background, you can see tourists (near right and in the distance in the upper left) stopping out of curiosity. There's enough of the distinctive architecture and signature ferns in the background to tip knowledgeable viewers off to the fact that the setting is the French Quarter, which markets itself as carnivalesque and fun.

Architectural Photography

Architectural photography seeks to emphasize and explain the aesthetic qualities of buildings and other man-made structures. Because of this emphasis on aesthetics of something carefully constructed, the images in architectural photography tend to be almost geometrically abstract to expose the lines or craftsmanship of a building. In *Down in the Crypt, Saint Gilles-du-Gard, France*, taken in the crypt of a Romanesque church, 56
I wanted to bring out the telescoping quality of the series of arches in the room. The Art Nouveau ironwork on the hand-rail of the ramp (and its shadow on the left wall) contributed leading lines to take the viewer into the deepest focal point of the image. The lighting is strong enough to show the elegant, smooth brickwork.

Architectural photography can also show how a building bore out its uses, or how it affected its human occupants. In *Slave Cabin, Whitney Plantation, Louisiana*, I placed the worn fence in front of the cabin to underscore the cabin as a place of imprisonment. The strong verticals of the fence act in agreement

▲ *Down in the Crypt, Saint Gilles-du-Gard*
◀ *Slave Cabin, Whitney Plantation, Louisiana*
Roman Aqueduct, Segovia, Spain ▶

with the porch supports, and the worn surfaces of the wood bespeak the cheap, disinterested craftsmanship that was never aimed at creating a comfortable environment for the people it housed.

The ancient *Roman Aqueduct, Segovia, Spain*, literally towers over the people who live there today. This architectural photo emphasizes the endless rhythm of the archways, which were constructed without mortar and yet still stand nearly two millennia later. The medieval buildings to the right are dwarfed by the superior construction, and the shadow that covers them works thematically to suggest that these buildings, while attractive and enduring, don't live up to the architectural and technological triumph of the monumental Roman structure.

A subgenre of architectural photography is real-estate photography, which is a commercial endeavor to make a structure appealing so that someone will want to buy it. As such, real-estate photography often uses wide-angle lenses, which makes small spaces seem bigger, and bright fill-in lighting to make rooms appear cheery and inviting. An exterior shot of a house may be taken from a low angle, to make it seem spacious, or be cropped to emphasize particularly attractive features that might be lost in a view of the whole facade of a house.

In *All Are Welcome, Saint Paul, Minnesota*, the porch lights give a warm feel to the front of the house even in broad daylight, and the enclosed porch is cropped to make it cozy but also to show the century-old woodwork that frames it. This close-up of the entry way is meant to convey, "Wouldn't you love to walk into this beautiful space and call it 'home'"?

▲ *All Are Welcome, Saint Paul, Minnesota*
Medieval Cat and Mouse, Poitiers, France ◥
Etruscan Chimera, Florence, Italy ▶

Documentary/Archival Photography

This genre of photography is often employed for museums or for scholarly purposes. Its goal is to render a subject clearly and accurately, so that the viewer can examine the subject in detail and learn from it—the next best thing to being in the subject's actual presence. Because of this need for accuracy, documentarian and archival photography is usually performed, if not in a real photography studio, then in the museum or repository where the subject dwells, and studio accessories are brought in for the shoot. Photographers documenting an item for a catalog or a textbook will use lenses noted for their capacity for sharpness as well as for their ability to function in low light without flash (in cases in which an object could be damaged by professional lighting). Tripods, reflectors, movable lights (where permissible), scaffolding (if an object is larger than miniature or human scale)—all of these are meticulously staged to create the best quality image possible with the least distortion.

The choir-stall carving in *Medieval Cat and Mouse, Poitiers, France*, couldn't be removed from its structure, which was over ten feet high and twenty feet long. I didn't have permission to use a tripod or additional lighting. My objective was to capture the figure in sharp enough detail that the fine nuances of the carving were visible—the rat's face, the cat's feet, and the way the grain of the wood affected the three dimensionality of the bas-relief. The bronze sculpture of a chimera in *Etruscan Chimera, Florence, Italy*, was well-lit because light would not damage it. Being in a situation in which I had no opportunity for scaffolding, nor a lot of space to get sufficient distance on all sides, I did my best to capture all three heads in reasonably sharp focus. I make my own photographs for educational purposes because many museum- or archive-issued photos are very old (and therefore of poor resolution for online or projection-screen uses) or expensive to obtain. As well, a museum-issued image may not be cropped or altered because it is the licensed intellectual property of the institution. Where permissions to shoot are possible, educators and scholars will endeavor to create their own quality images for instruction.

Portraiture Photography

Portraiture photography is a large part of the professional industry. Individuals and groups want their own high-quality—and even better-than-real—images of themselves or loved ones for posterity, to commemorate life events, or to advertise themselves as professionals (often known as "head shots"). Some portraiture photography is enhanced, so that the subjects look more like the people they see in movies or magazines; this photography is not about realism (which might be seen in portraits done for newspapers) but about idealizing or styling subjects as they would like to appear—better than real.

This form of photography, though usually done by professionals, is so popular that social media and cellphones have filters that individuals can use to achieve highly stylized looks. Professional portraiture usually requires a good amount of equipment to achieve a flattering effect—not just background drapes, large lights, diffusers, reflectors, tripods, and the like, but also very sophisticated post-production editing equipment, like Photoshop, to even out skin tone, correct blemishes, and tame stray hair, just for starters. Portraiture photographers are sensitive to angles: shooting subjects from below may make them imposing, but the resulting shadows and potential distortion of features could be very unflattering. In *Lynette*, I didn't do any major retouching, but I chose to photograph the subject from above, so that the roadbed behind her acted as a neutral, framing background. The even light of the overcast day acted as a natural diffuser to keep harsh shadows or strong light off her face.

▲ *Lynette*

The Music Man ▶

knowing that many relatives will be receiving copies of their shot—the senior photo is a rite of passage, and taking such photos well requires great personal and technical skill).

Portraiture photographers may include other objects in the frame in order to give a viewer clues about how subjects see themselves or are seen by others in the world. In *The Music Man*, I pulled back from the subject's captivating face to include both the objects that surrounded him in musical instrument shop and in which he took pride and his t-shirt, which speaks of his hometown loyalty.

Wedding photographers have to capture the customers' fantasy of what their day means, coordinate all the relatives and friends who will be in the shot, all on a very compressed schedule, with no do-overs for mistakes. They have to perfectly execute the expected standard shots

Portraiture photographers have to develop good interpersonal skills to make a subject comfortable enough to have a natural or pleasant expression. Subjects must trust the photographer to put them in their best possible light (such as in senior photos, in which a young person wants to look adult and handsome, (first dance, cutting the cake, couple with bridesmaids and bridegrooms), as well as innovate ways to make the day seem unique and cinematic.

Abstract Photography

This genre of photography is so vast that it is almost too much to encapsulate in a brief entry here. Abstract photography deliberately alters items within its frame to produce artificial effects, taking images far from the realm of realism. Some abstract photographers specialize in manipulating the printing process to provide unusual textures and distortions; others may treat the surface of film to create effects; most common is to use computer tools to introduce colors, shapes, or kinds of focus that turn the original image into an interesting study of geometry or tonal range. A very common method of abstract photography is to take a real object but frame it devoid of its ordinary context or scale. A photographer with access to drones or a plane can photograph a place from such a high perspective that it can't be recognized as the place, but becomes an unfamiliar pattern.

In *Golden Frost*, I took a macro shot of ice patterns on a window but shot them with a shallow depth of field, which blurred out the sunny house behind. I then cropped the ice to appear many times larger than it would appear to someone looking out the window.

To varying degrees, abstract photographers may include something recognizable in the frame. Photography that deliberately manipulates a recognizable scene for mood or special effect can be discerned from abstraction by the degree to which the image appears to be more about its style than its ability to narrate a story.

62

▲ *Golden Frost*

Romantic Ranunculus ▶

Fine-Art Photography

This genre, too, is so wide and varied that it defies a comprehensive description here. The simplest definition is that fine-art photography seeks to be judged primarily on its aesthetic qualities. While all the genres described here have merits based on their beauty, the criteria for value in fine-art photography lie in an image's appeal to the viewer as "art" (another very broad and elastic term). Because of the broad sweep of the genre, any sort of equipment can be used, from the most expensive and complicated to the most basic (your cellphone, for instance, although these cameras are becoming quite sophisticated).

Sometimes a photograph from journalism, science, or documentary can become so admired and so frequently reproduced that it is lifted from its original category and is understood foremost as art. Aesthetic appeal can derive from the photograph's style, its innovation in representing its subject, or its ability to strip something mundane down to geometric or abstract parts. In these instances, the photograph calls attention to the photographer's creativity more than to the subject found in the creation. Reading a fine art photograph on its own terms requires a decision about what qualities will be used in the evaluation, and that choice can be quite individual. One person may want art that is soothing or sentimental or which satisfies a particular palette; another may want art that is provocative or which rejects conventional definitions of beauty for drama or an emphasis on concept over beauty.

Flower studies and still lifes are well-established in the tradition of fine art photography. With *Romantic Ranunculus*, I wanted to evoke the mood and style of still lifes done by Dutch and Flemish painters in the sixteenth century. I backed away from a tack-sharp, ultra-realistic shot of the photos and instead sought to create something that was softer and moodier in lighting and texture while clearly representative of the subject. I used candlelight on the left and sunlight diffused through an ivory window shade on the right to create some blur and a muting of

the intense colors of the *Ranunculus*. This image meets the criteria for fine-art photography in that its emphasis is of the beauty of the light and the sensual delicacy of the petals. There's nothing particularly fitting for nature or documentarian genres here—it is too dim and too soft for a view that seeks to reveal facts from close examination of the subject

Ode to Sally Mann, too, is better suited to being categorized as fine-art photography. The photo's approach to its subjects is enigmatic and captures a quality of childhood—curiosity and exploration—more than it speaks to portraiture (the subjects' identities are not explored). By virtue of the natural setting and lack of narrative in the image, photojournalism or street photography can be ruled out. The aesthetic appeal is in concept and composition. Black-and-white photography gets the viewer's attention precisely because it is not how humans see. Whereas a color photo could look so close to reality that it renders a subject mundane, portraying the same subject in black-and-white calls attention to texture, placement, and shadings that otherwise could be ignored

Black-and-White Photography

Fans and many practitioners of black-and-white photography feel that this genre is an art form unto itself. While the beginnings of photography were primarily black-and-white because the chemical processing of silver-gelatin film was relatively inexpensive and manageable, color photography existed in the nineteenth century, but the affordability and availability of color today has not destroyed the appeal of black-and-white. Black-and-white images are made, sold, and appreciated in all genres of photography.

In photojournalism, black-and-white lends a kind of gravitas to its subjects, drawing on a long tradition of text books and archives that use black-and-white photos either of necessity (such photos were common in the past) or for consistency of representation. Black-and-white, in this genre, bespeaks history and formality. For portraiture, black-and-white lends the subject a romantic moodiness (dark shadows, tonal contrasts) and a seriousness that comes from the long tradition of black-and-white photos as "high art." Travel photographers may use black-and-white for these purposes, too, in rendering a portrait of a place. For all of the genres in this chapter, black-and-white is valued for removing color as a distractor, leaving in its place an emphasis on pattern, geometry, and composition. Architectural and street photographers want you to see the lines and structure of places. Nature photographers (especially those using macro) use black-and-white to bring out details that may be obscured by striking color.

For years, standard instructional procedure in the field of photography was to start students with black and white, allowing them to focus on compositional technique. The thinking was that color would keep students thinking about the subject or scene, and they would not be as conscious of how they were composing their shots because their minds would fill-in information or focus that was not really in the frame. Black-and-white images would be just abstract enough for the student to pay attention to items in a frame as discrete objects, to stop interpreting what appeared through the viewfinder as reality, and to start thinking about the image as art they could craft consciously.

Ode to Sally Mann

Our Lady of Autun, France, is one of my favorite images: a nouveau-Romanesque sculpture of Mary Magdalene at Autun Cathedral. My first photography professor would always ask us, when we submitted work for critique, "Do you think this is a photo of a beautiful thing or a beautiful photo?" I wanted the answer to be both, but the implicit lesson was important: "What are you bringing to the subject? Are you relying on the subject to carry the picture instead of on your skills?"

▲ *Our Lady of Autun, France*

This statue, a gray item in a dark portico, registered in color as much more mundane. In color, the image was washed out or drab—when we see color, we really want to see it and, if it's too obscured, we feel we're seeing a poorly-exposed image. In black-and-white, the high contrast of light and dark are virtues, not defects. The blackness of the shadows creates a mood, and what is lit seems to be in a spotlight. The black/white/grays of the picture bring out every line of the drapery and of Mary's hair, making this photo a study in lines and curves. Black-and-white takes this from a dim, dull image without much interest to a dramatic one in which every detail shines out as beautiful. Because I was able to choose an angle for isolating the statue from others and could use the right exposure to permit both deep shadows and bright lights, I feel I succeeded in taking a beautiful photo of a beautiful thing.

Fashion Photography, Stock Photography, and Sports Photography

These genres are arguably among the most omnipresent and lucrative types of photography today. Fashion photography is often aligned with fine-art photography because its aesthetic appeal is central to its creation; however, fashion photography is first and last about selling clothing. It does far more than show one what clothing looks like; it frequently equates clothing with a lifestyle, with an identity that the viewer personally desires, and offers clothing as integral to assuming that identity. Fashion photography is known for its use of models, and some models do become famous faces and bodies that are branded as a lifestyle in themselves.

When sellers associate a recognizable face with their clothing, they are trying to tie merchandise to glamour and individuality. In these instances, fashion photographers may use conventions associated with portraiture, but they don't do so for the purpose of revealing an individual. Instead, fashion photography creates a simulacrum of a portrait—the model is presented in close-up, with great attention to and flattering of her or his face and body but, in reality, the individuality is a fiction built to sell the brand or merchandise. Models, even supermodels whose names are well known, are usually selected for their excellence as a type, not their unique appearance.

Models are generally selected for being much thinner and taller than the average consumer, with regular facial features that can appear mask-like. Indeed, in fashion shows and advertisements, models are styled with heavy makeup and unusual hairstyles and hair colors, and they are instructed to display particular expressions, making them more a canvas in an ad than a distinctive person. Nonetheless, fashion photography is loved for its innovation and dramatic excellence because it makes mass-produced commercial items seem special, unique, and powerful. Serious high-end fashion photography requires lots of studio equipment (movable lights, high stationary lights, backdrapes to isolate the subject, top-quality cameras with a range of lenses for different effects), not to mention a budget for hair and makeup professionals—and expensive models.

Stock photography is a lot like fashion photography in that the subject is usually imagined as a canvas for what a seller may want to create upon it. Stock photography attempts to thread the needle between being strikingly attractive and inoffensively generic at the same time. The goal of stock photographers is to create an image that can be used in as many different venues by as many different clients as possible.

Clients seeking stock photos are generally trying to save money in devising their own advertising campaigns, so they seek photos with a pleasing amount of negative space where print can be layered onto an image and be clearly seen. Or they want to spare the expense of paying their own models. Stock-photography catalogs give clients a wide range of models across race, age, and appearance, already skillfully lit and shot, at a fraction of the cost of funding a dedicated ad campaign by an advertising agency.

Looking at stock photos and trying to express how they are different from other genres of photos is a valuable exercise. Where the stock photographer wants to downplay an individual artistic style, a portrait or street photographer seeks to emphasize it in order to develop both exceptional skill and a reputation. Stock photography can be very lucrative, and some stock photographers have multi-million-dollar businesses with expensive studios and equipment. Within those studios, ironically, they are intent on creating images that will act as background for others' content rather than calling the viewer's attention to the artistry of their work.

Sports photography is, like fashion photography, known for its drama and for its famous faces. The key difference is that sports photography, unlike fashion or stock photography, must follow action rather than stage it. The sports photographer needs very fast cameras with long-range lenses that work well in low light (a sports venue may seem brightly lit, but when viewed down a long telephoto barrel, it becomes quite dim). To freeze the action of a key moment from a game, a photographer needs blisteringly rapid shutter speeds and fast, synchronized flash equipment. The long lens and the need for a fast shutter speed make for a challenging combination, and this makes great skill and a strong flash system all the more important. Sports photographers have to get their shot the first time (although they can use continuous shooting to make multiple images per second, in the hopes that one will come out). Because they are shooting subjects where historical veracity is important (frequently, this genre is linked with photojournalism), they cannot usually manipulate images much beyond cropping or light balance.

Because of expense and professional preference, I do not do any of these types of photography, and cannot give you personal examples, but I trust that the ubiquity of examples of these genres in mass media will allow you to consider images created by others in terms of the descriptions written here.

Composition

Composition is the overall arrangement of elements in a frame. In any photo, the relationship of items to each other and the effect those relationships have to one another can be described. Examples may illustrate this better than words.

In *The Santa Marta Offering, Marta, Italy*, there are arguably two elements/figures in the frame: the bull and the man. The composition here puts the bull in the foreground, occupying two thirds of the frame, with the man in the far-right third. The sun on the bull's white hide and the red tassels on its horns contrast strikingly with the man's black coat and hat and with his face (in shadow). The bull dominates the composition, but the man's striking contrast to the bull lends him visual weight. Because the bull is shot in close-up, he nearly fills the frame; however, his uniformly white coat acts almost as negative space. When the eye travels to the right of the frame for more detail, it lands on the man: his face is the most expressive and detailed element for the eye to work on. The composition of this photo can be described in terms of proportional relationships between the two figures.

Bridge Over the River Trebbia, Bobbio, Italy, is another example. The elements in the frame could be listed as sky, bridge, riverbed, and town. The bridge dominates the foreground and acts as a leading line to the town. The sky is the brightest element of the frame and forms a triangle that

Bridge Over the River Trebbia, Bobbio, Italy ▶
Fern Vectors ◤
▼ *The Santa Maria Offering, Marta, Italy*

68

Strong compositions direct the audience to one or two focal points and present some sort of engaging relationship between elements in the frame. In cases in which there is one element (say a portrait subject), the lack of unrelated or distracting elements in the frame allows the viewer to concentrate on the intriguing details of a single subject (arguably its own mix of elements.

contrasts with the one formed by the dark bridge. The arches in the bridge have a rhythm as they recede into the frame. The riverbed acts as a horizon line for the other elements.

In *Fern Vectors*, a photo that looks to be all of a piece, the elements in the frame start to stand out from each other as abstract geometry. Here, you have either one thing—a patch of leaves, or several—upwards of twenty fronds or dozens of individual leaves. The stems create many diverging lines, and the placement of the frond in the top left corner comes in perpendicularly to most of the other fronds, almost perfectly overlapping the stem. The stem acts as a spine for the neatly alternating fronds that continue traveling diagonally in a line across the frame to the lower right corner. The replicating rhythms of the individual fronds in each leaf create vectors out of the frame on either side of the diagonal made by the main stem. The elements in the frame could be seen either as boringly repetitive or jarringly chaotic (because they all point in different directions outside the frame, giving the eye no place to anchor), but the perpendicular frond is slightly in the foreground and contrasts with the shadows beneath it, giving the eye a place to land before it travels about.

Subject

A figure or object that appears to be the most important visual element in a photo's frame is referred to as "the subject" or "the dominant." When a photo contains many elements (especially if they seem to be the same size or similarly lit) the subject may be difficult to discern, or the photo may take more than one item as a collective subject.

When a viewer searches a photo for its dominant subject, the decision-making process can include constructing the meaning or intention of the photo. The vocabulary introduced in this text will give you clues for arriving at the subject in a photo and for constructing meaning once you find one.

▲ *Flaming Redhead*
Aster Cafe, Saint Paul, Minnesota ▼

In *Flaming Redhead*, the dominant is the figure in the foreground. The figure is facing us, is the only full face we see, and is in the sharpest focus. She is on the first "third" in the Rule of Thirds, and is the most dramatically lit by the fire.

The subject of a photo is not always as clear as in the above example. An image that has multiple in-focus figures, or no obviously differentiated figure, might seem to have no subject at all. When you encounter an image like this, it is often rewarding to take a little time to read the composition for clues.

In *Aster Cafe, Saint Paul, Minnesota*, one human subject can be seen in the far background and not in sharp focus. The room is empty of people but full of many pieces of furniture, fixtures, and architectural features. The double-doors in the background, with the arched windows, are centered in the composition. They do act as a frame-within-a-frame for the walking figure, but the visual weight of the figure isn't strong enough to hold the viewer's focus. A lone glass catches the sunlight on a table nearly dead-center in the room, but its scale is too small for the glass to register strongly in the image. Different pieces of furniture are in focus, and the light strikes them engagingly but, again, nothing seems to dominate.

At this point in looking, then, a good strategy would be to consider the composition as a whole. Perhaps the room itself is the subject, with its vintage furniture, brick walls, old lamps and candles, and bare floor which evoke a time period that contrasts with the parked car and modern-dressed walker outside. While the items in the photo are all recognizable, the overall set of leading lines going up and down, curving, and at different diagonals suggest that this photo can function as an abstract composition. Looking to genre as a guide, the likeliest candidates seem to be architectural, documentary, or art photography (black and white is a given). Photojournalism or travel as genres seem weaker options because of the lack of action or identifying information.

The subject of this photo may be debatable, but parameters for identifying the subject include composition, style, and indicators of genre. The guide that most viewers look to, however, is captioning, expecting words from the publisher, editor, or photographer to guide their interpretation of the image. Captioning can be essential to reading a photojournalistic or documentarian photo because these photos are often placed in journals, newspapers, blogs, or historical films/books to inform the viewer of some truth. This is not to say, however, that captions can't be (mis)leading or politically subjective. A viewer educated in photographic composition has tools to arrive at personal, informed decisions.

Foreground/Background

The earlier "planar perspective" section dealt with this idea in some detail, but the terms "foreground" and "background" are more commonly used and need some addressing here. Most photos that are not artistic abstractions or scientific renderings (like an X-ray or an MRI scan) convey a representation of elements that are recognizable as existing in three dimensions. Thus, some elements will appear to be in front of or behind others, suggesting depth. Foreground and background also exist as theatrical concepts (sometimes expressed as "upstage" and "downstage") which highlight the photographer's hand in staging a photograph in order to emphasize some elements more than others. In *Athena Checks Out Pan, Getty Museum, Los Angeles*, these concepts are

72   plainly rendered: the onyx statue is in the foreground, and the white marble statue is in the background. Note, however, that just because an element is in the foreground does not require that it be the main subject. The onyx statue acts as a frame for the white statue in the background, creating a strong contrast to direct the eye. If the black statue had been removed, the statue in the background would have been dwarfed by all the negative space around it.

In *The Ferocious Candelabrum*, the foreground element is the focus of the photo, but that doesn't mean that the element in the background is irrelevant. The panther carving at the front of the antique candelabrum shows the figure frontally and in sharp focus, but the slightly blurred panther carving in the background affords a profile (or nearly so) view, giving the viewer a fuller appreciation of the skill of the work.

▲ *Athena Checks Out Pan, Getty Museum, Los Angeles*
The Ferocious Candelabrum ▶

Rule of Thirds

This concept is probably the composition advice that is most often handed out to photography students. In fact, the "Rule of Thirds" is attributed to a painter, John Thomas Smith, who published it in 1797, forty years before photography was invented. Smith's contention was that if one were to set up six imaginary lines on an image, three at regularly spaced intervals horizontally and three vertically, the most compelling composition would result from situating the main subject of the composition on the intersection of one set of those lines. While this rule is not absolute, it does often work, and it is demonstrable that subjects centered in a frame can look very static and plain, like a mug shot or driver's license photo. When reading photos, you may look to see if the Rule of Thirds is in play, and whether it is an ingredient in the strength of the composition.

74

   Fountain Abbey Ruins, England, is a photo of an empty room, but framing the shot so that the window is slightly to the right of center opens up a rhythmic pattern in the architecture, creating more energy in the shot. If I had stood directly in front of the window, the expanse of dirt between the camera and the window would have been more noticeable and more boring.

   In *Enkidu in Rainbows,* the cat is in the right-hand third of the image. His gaze from his side of the frame to a vector off to the left-side of the image makes the eye travel with his gaze. If he had occupied the middle of the frame, the busy architectural features in the background would have framed him and made him seem smaller.

▲ *The Reach, Lake Como, Saint Paul, Minnesota*

Aziz, the Andalusian Lion ▶

In the final shot, *The Reach, Lake Como, Saint Paul, Minnesota*, the tree's expanse travels from the background of the upper-left third of the frame to the foreground of the lower-right third. The tree has more detail in its two ends than in the middle, and the arrival of the eye from one end to the other gives the image a more dynamic sense. If the

tree had been completely vertical and had simply bisected the frame, the shot would look prosaic and unthoughtful.

Scale

Because a camera can frame a subject of almost any size and isolate it from its context, photography can play with scale in a manner that surprises and delights a viewer. In journalistic or documentarian photography, a chief goal is to give viewers visual cues that allow them to know the real-world size of an object. Thus, in archeology, objects are photographed with measuring rods called "photo scales" to tell a viewer the exact size of an item that is typically isolated on a plain background.

In general, scale can be defined as the proportional relationship of objects that gives a viewer clues to their relative size. If you photograph a blue ball next to a soda can, a viewer who has experience with the dimensions of a real-life soda can is able to grasp the size of the ball. Three types of scale that are typically invoked in photography are monumental scale (elements in the frame express massive size), human scale (non-massive elements appear to be represented as in proportion to how a person experiences the real world), and miniature scale (elements appear smaller than when people encounter them in real life).

Photographers like to play and surprise, so they often play with the convention of scale. The eleventh-century statuette from Andalusia in *Aziz, the Andalusian Lion* is a favorite at the Minneapolis Institute of the Arts. In its creation, the goldsmith played with scale, taking a large predator and rendering him toy-sized: barely six inches high. In this photo, I've reversed the effect

by isolating the lion from any objects in the frame that would give an idea of his actual size and framing him so that he takes up two-thirds of the photo. In so doing, his scale is larger than it might seem. I photographed him using the conventions of monumental scale (including situating him so that his entire body doesn't fit into the frame), even though the statue is anything but monumental. The photo was shot with a macro lens, which presented the statue as larger than in real life (in an eight-inch by ten-inch frame).

Macrophotography, as discussed in the Distortion segment, draws much of its power from taking things of extremely tiny scale and rendering them literally larger than life (often many times so).

Scale can also be manipulated to make massive things seem smaller, even if they are represented at the size humans encounter them. In *Beaux Arts Modernist Funhouse*, a larger building offers a reflection of a smaller one. With this photo, I wanted to convey the passing of a particular era of architecture, so I looked for a striking way to show the diminishment of the older style. I found a Beaux Arts-style building next to a modern skyscraper whose facade was almost entirely mirrored. I used the design elements of the modernist building to frame the Beaux Arts structure. The angle of the glass tiles, and their multiple small squares, disrupt the image, breaking the older building into small pieces and distort-

Beaux Arts Modernist Funhouse ▶

ing its individual elements. Framing a building contains and dwarfs its monumental scale, suggesting that the structure can be encapsulated by an even larger one. Frame-within-in-frame is a common art technique used to direct the eye by isolating and emphasizing a particular part of an image. Usually, frame-within-frame succeeds in pulling an object into greater importance. In this photo, however, frame-within-frame subverted the audience's understanding of a monumental (literally) subject by diminishing that subject.

Miniature scale is common in aerial or long-distance shots. *Manarola Noir, Cinque Terre, Italy*, shows two human figures against the ground of the hill they are descending. From the raised perspective of the camera, the figures seem tiny and their features are indeterminate, not just because they are in shadow but also because they are far away.

79

The smallness of these walkers is further emphasized by the long shadows they cast in the single streetlight. The relative scale of objects around them makes them the smallest things in the frame. They are dwarfed by the engulfing, black negative space that surrounds them in the frame, the shadowed wall on the left, the road rising high behind them, and the fishing boats that read as bigger than they are because they are arranged on a rising incline.

◀ *Manarola Noir, Cinque Terre, Italy*

Leading Lines

Elements in the composition of a photo can direct the eyes to rest or focus on a particular part of the image. While an image like a passport photo or a product in a catalog typically places a solitary object in the center of the frame, with no other elements competing for attention, the photographer can frame other photos to create a trajectory for the viewer's gaze.

In *Girona Courtyard, Spain*, the serpentine bench enters from the lower left of the frame and curves toward the archway in the center. If I had moved several feet to the right to take a photo of just the arch, the vast, plain expanse of the stone walkway would have made much of the image uninteresting and uniform. The archway as the central vanishing point is preserved in this shot, but the curving bench encourages the eye to arrive there by a more energetic path.

Staircases are excellent for creating leading lines. In *Wells Cathedral Staircase, England*, the staircase is unusual because it branches in two different directions near the top. Nonetheless, the steps, though they are worn to the point of irregularity, lead the viewer from the lower part of the image up to the central archway.

Girona Courtyard, Spain ▼

There are numerous sets of lines in this image: the ribs of the vaulting in the ceiling and the archivolts in the Gothic arch above the door and on the upper-left side of the passageway. However, the strong, regular, and visually weighty rhythm of the stairs is the element that directs the eye most strongly. Leading lines don't have to lead to the single-point focus of an image. Sometimes leading lines can create vectors that point out of the frame or simply produce a rhythm that creates a pleasurable pattern for the eye to pursue. The lines of the leaves of the plant in *Butterfly Bush* arc away from each other, but their regular, receding intervals suggest depth in the image, creating a pattern that moves out horizontally to either side of the frame but also travels up vertically in a way that seems to head inward.

▼ *Butterfly Bush*
Wells Cathedral Staircase, England ▲

Figure-to-Ground

Figure-to-ground describes the power of high contrast between elements in an image. As a result, one element is emphasized in importance as a subject. The "figure" is an object that seems framed clearly against a non-detailed area (the "ground"). The ground acts as negative space that highlights the figure. The presence of a high-contrast figure-to-ground relationship in a frame draws the viewer's eye to rest longer on that figure because the contrast endows it with visual weight. This concept has its origins in painting but has been used to great effect by photographers as well.

In *On the Sagrada Catwalk*, numerous people appear in the foreground, but they do not spring forth as subjects—not because they are dark or out of focus (although this helps), but because they are not rendered as figures in high contrast to a ground. The "ground" area of the photo makes the subject (figure) clearly visible. Think of it as a frame-within-frame. The walker in this photo is in the back plane of the image. She is in focus, but she is just as dark (if not darker) than the people in the foreground. What makes her stand out is that she is walking toward a white wall on which a lot of light is shining. Though there are larger, closer, and more colorful elements in the frame all about her, she stands out. If she were walking in front of the brown door to her left (like the woman in the foreground who is directly in front of it), she would lose her high contrast frame, be harder to see, and lose the visual weight that allows her to be the focus of the image.

On the Sagrada Catwalk ▲

▲ *Blurred Timelines in Conques, France*

The high-contrast figure-to-ground effect can be achieved with light items on a dark background as well. The contrast in *Blurred Timelines in Conques*, France, isn't as clean as in the preceding photo, but the novice's white cassock stands out against the building because he is in full sunlight and the entrance is in full shade. Note, however, that his dark hair doesn't contrast enough with the doorway, and this causes the detail of his head to be lost in the exposure. This greatly reduces the impact of the photo, but there is enough striking contrast in the figure and clarity in the dark regions that a full figure is present as the subject.

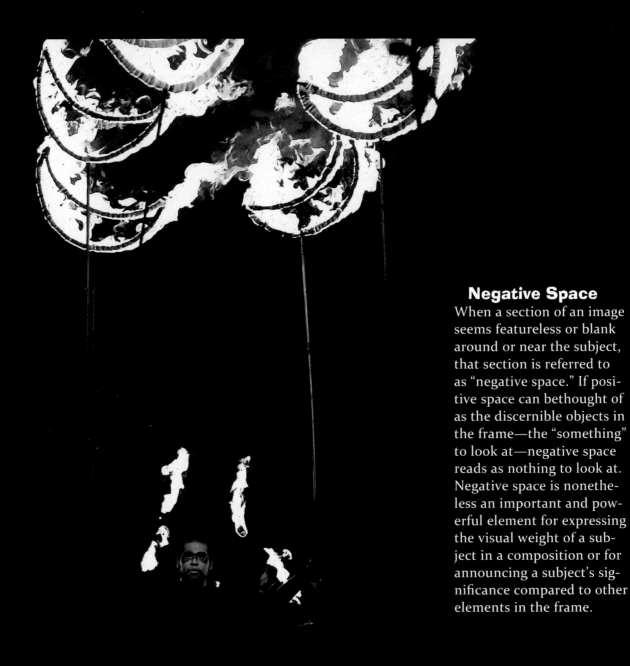

Negative Space

When a section of an image seems featureless or blank around or near the subject, that section is referred to as "negative space." If positive space can bethought of as the discernible objects in the frame—the "something" to look at—negative space reads as nothing to look at. Negative space is nonetheless an important and powerful element for expressing the visual weight of a subject in a composition or for announcing a subject's significance compared to other elements in the frame.

The subject of *Flame Thrower, Saint Paul, Minnesota*, is almost invisible because the lighting supplied by the fire he wields is too weak to bring his whole body into view. His head and shoulders seem to hover in space. Because the fire is so amorphous, his face is the most detailed and recognizable thing we can look at.

The negative space almost overwhelms him as a subject, but it also literally highlights him because he's the only thing visible besides the fire.

The sky can be said to be the negative space around the medieval tower in *Medieval Tower, Fiesole, Italy*. Because the tower is so strongly silhouetted, however, the true "story" of this photo could be the amazing color of the sky, and the black areas could be understood as a kind of negative space that helps frame how vivid that sky is. Without the near-featureless tower and trees in the foreground, the sky might not even register as sky. It is so vast and formless that another element in the composition is needed to focus the attention there.

...trait photographers use plain backdrops or background curtains for similar reasons. The medieval sculp... ...on of Christ, *Twelfth Century, National Art Museum of Catalunya, Barcelona, Spain*, stands before a blank... ...d key lighting shines on the sculpture, allowing the negative space to hold the sculpture up for detailed vi... ...production, I removed the shadows on the wall so the negative space would be clean for the subject.

A photographer can make a choice to have no negative space in an image, filling the frame with the subject. The inlaid stone floor in *Cosmatesque Floor, Ravenna, Italy*, created a dizzying pattern with lots of high-contrast moments, particularly at the top of the frame where light from a door hit the tiles strongly. I framed the shot so that you could see the outermost edges of the circle in the upper left and right corners, but included nothing above the floor, which might have diminished its impact or distract from the pattern. Arguably, one could say that the pattern itself in the floor is a series of figure-to-ground elements in overwhelming succession.

Separation of Subject

"Separation of subject" is another way to analyze the sharpness and convincing depth of field of an in-focus section in an image. Separation of subject can boost the clarity of the main point of interest in a photo by making it stand out. Zoom lenses can have problems with separation of focus because they compress distance in a frame; even though everything in the frame is in focus, it can be difficult to tell how far behind the main subject other elements actually are.

Many photographers try to frame a subject carefully so that items in the background don't seem to extrude from it (when leaning a subject against a tree or light pole, for example, making sure that the tree/pole doesn't seem to be growing out of the subject's head). They may achieve this through planning for a strong figure-to-ground contrast. The weaker a contrast between subject and background, the flatter (and perhaps less interesting) a subject will seem.

88

Not much contrast exists between the background and the medieval statue in *Medieval Mary, Toulouse, France*. The gray of the wall is similar in shade to the gray of the saint, although key lighting from the upper left throws the statue into sharper relief. I also actively blurred the background in post-production to strengthen the contrast in clarity between the subject and the wall. While the tonal range of the photo is pretty narrow (true whites and true blacks are in short supply), the subject is fairly strongly separated from its background.

In the portrait in *His Dark Materials*, I wanted to create poor subject separation in order to contribute to a mysterious atmosphere. The only three-dimensional clarity for the subject is on the side of him closest to the window. His eyeglasses, nose, hair, and shoulder emerge from the gloom, but the rest of his face fades into invisibility.

▲ *Medieval Mary, Toulouse, France*
His Dark Materials ▶

◀ *Lake Como Carousel, Saint Paul, Minnesota*

Sagrado Dog, Barcelona, Spain ▼

The overlapping figures of the carousel horses in *Lake Como Carousel, Saint Paul, Minnesota* create some distraction from the front horse, even though the first horse is sharpest in focus. Most of the foreground is sharp and in high contrast, especially the light glancing off the breastplate of the horse tack, which creates greater definition from the second horse at a point at which they would otherwise be a similar register of gray. The subject separation breaks down a little around the nostrils and forelock of the front horse, making the subject a little harder to pick out. The raised head of the third horse (upper-right corner), and the lowered nose of the fourth one (lower middle-right) are poorly separated because they, too, closely match the other dark gray elements near them.

A very sharp camera lens with a small aperture will create strong separation of subject, even if the subject is of the same material as its background. The dog sculpture in *Sagrado Dog, Barcelona, Spain*, is part of a large statuary ensemble high up on a wall, but enough deep-relief carving is visible to create contrasting shadows in the stone. The lens and the small aperture are what allow the sculpture to stand out crisply. Even though this photo is in color, the stone of the building's facade and the dog sculpture are all in the same tonal range. The dog, however, does not blend into the background. There is just enough shadow to create differentiation on the left corner of wall, and the difference in texture of the wall also creates contrast. The camera renders the carving sharply enough to make clear at all points that the dog is part of neither the wall nor the stones beneath. Because of this, you can clearly identify the subject of the photo.

91

Distortion

Different types of camera lenses bend the light that reaches the camera sensor in ways that photographers can use as tools for creating particular effects. Most commonly, a wide-angle lens will bend the content at the edges of the frame as it reaches for a broad capture. Some of these effects can be corrected in digital post-production to render a more natural-looking subject, but the requisite compressions of the frame usually mean cropping the photo a great deal.

Often photographers embrace these unrealistic effects. In *Pantheon, Rome, Italy*, for example, the massive circular dome of the Pantheon and its oculus are visible. Because of the scale of the subject, a 50mm lens either can't take it all in or must be used from near the floor, causing the roof to recede. The result is a loss of the scale that was the very reason for taking the photo. My wide-angle lens bent the circular dome into a pronounced oval. Because of the strong leading line where the roof meets the dome's base, and the rhythm of the coffered ceiling (which diminishes the size of the recesses as they get closer to the oculus), the distortion of the subject creates a spiraling effect. Even though this dome is perfectly symmetrical and round in real life, the lens pulls the image from top-left to bottom-right, making the concentric circles of the coffers appear to spiral. Not a desirable effect for a documentarian or journalistic representation, but it is visually interesting as art photography.

and their arches seem to lean inward to converge: this is an example of keystoning. The focus on the vaulting from the foreground to the apse in the background also seems to indicate that the ceiling lines start wide and angle inward toward a vanishing point at the back. This gives the subject a kind of funhouse-mirror effect, but the receding rhythmic lines suggest the distance in time that has passed since the creation of the building, evoking themes of history and eternity.

Pantheon, Rome, Italy
Notre-Dame de Paris, France, Interior ▼

Architectural photos often contain distortions because their massive scale necessitates a wide-angle lens. A building that is, of course, perpendicular to the ground will look as though it is leaning away from the viewer in a photo because of lens distortion. Even if the photographer uses a telephoto or 50mm lens (approximating human visual perspective), the camera sensor must be tilted away from the subject to include it all, and this is how distortion is exacerbated. Because of keystoning, if the camera is held at 30° away from the building, the relationship of the top of the sensor to the bottom will appear different. Photographers may avoid this with a tilt-shift lens (which is slanted to correct for distance differences between the top and bottom of a subject) or in digital post-production software. *Notre-Dame de Paris, Interior, France,* shows distortions front to back and side-to-side. The columns

94   When a human or human-like subject is photographed from below, the proportions of the body are distorted with respect to the way we understand them in a straight-on perspective. The sculpture in *Liberation* itself distorts the size of the hands of the figure to emphasize the theme, but that distortion effect is compounded when the subject is photographed from below with a wide-angle lens. The head, thrown back in jubilation, is tipped away from the camera and appears tiny. As a result, it is more distant from the camera than are the hands in the foreground. Again, this photo might be considered too inaccurate for use as documentation in a museum catalog, but, in the realm of fine art, the photographer's lens choice reinforces the theme and spirit of the work.

  It is easy to see the distortion of a wide-angle lens in subjects familiar to the audience. In *Pawing the Camera*, the housecat is in fairly normal proportions in the middle-plane of the image, and the diminishment of the back plane is less noticeable

▲ *Liberation*

◄ *Pawing the Camera*

because it is too dark for many defining details to emerge. But the extended paw in the foreground is obviously out of proportion to the rest of the cat, and it has intruded beyond the shallow focal plane of the lens (only the face of the cat is in sharp focus). The distortion is appealing because it surprises the viewer—something familiar and small pops forward as big—but it also reveals something about the personality of the cat, whose reach is greater than his small size.

  Macro lenses can distort quite differently from wide-angle lenses. Macro lenses often have a very slender depth of field, so only a part of even a tiny object may be in focus in the frame. Macro lenses also can render a subject larger than it is in life, which is one of the reasons many viewers find them so captivating. To see a tiny flower or bug fill a frame in the kind of detail that one never experiences with the naked eye is very compelling.

Macro lenses may seem to distort by recording images in this fashion, but they actually mimic a truth about our vision that our brain has taught us to ignore: we actually see only certain things in focus as we look at them, but we dismiss or fill-in our perceptions (and memories), certain that what we saw was entirely in focus. In reality, our eyes take several continuous "snapshots" of what they see, at varying focal points, and interpret them as all of a piece. The lampshades in *Shades of Gold* are less than three inches apart, but the macro lens, with its shallow depth-of-field, holds only the lip of the shade in the foreground in perfect focus. As the eye travels into the mid-plane and the back-plane of the image, the lines of the shades' rims grow less distinct.

Many kinds of distortions can be present in a photo—the result of lighting and composition choices—and I'll describe them in other sections.

▼ *Shades of Gold*

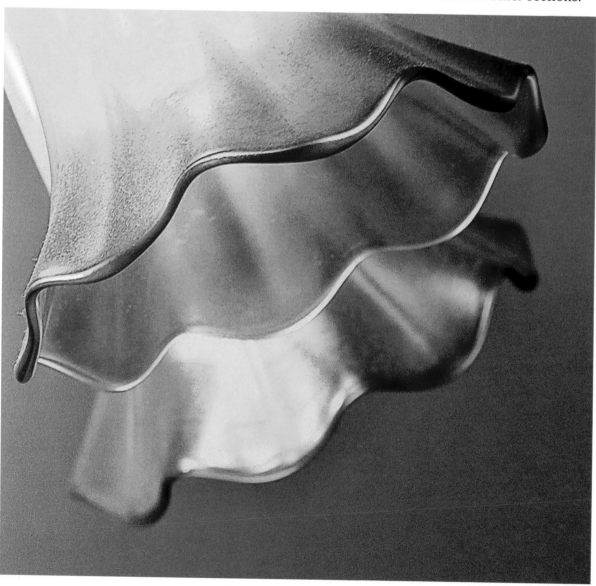

Context

Sometimes what a viewer wants to know in order to decide how to interpret a photo is its context: the conditions surrounding the composition and presentation of the image. In framing a shot, the photographer makes decisions about what to include and exclude from that context. Ruling objects out of the frame may be a matter of deeming them distractions from the main topic so that the focus of the viewer can be directed and narrowed.

The degree to which an image includes lesser-weighted objects that surround the subject is the degree to which that subject is contextualized. To convey that a subject is a musician, the photographer might include her instrument, or sheet music, or a microphone and a crowd. To explain a subject's distressed expression, the photographer might pull the camera back far enough to show a burning house or a war scene or a hospital room. A photo is sometimes framed so that the subject leads a viewer to think about what is not in the frame—a greater context. A photo of a bombed building might have a child's crushed toy in the foreground, provoking the viewer to wonder what happened to the residents of the building. When photographers use their photos to tell stories, they make decisions about what to place in a frame to suggest a point-of-view about the story, or what gave rise to the story, or where it might end. Context can be inside the

frame, or the items in the frame can call upon the viewer to ask questions about the context not included in the frame.

As these examples suggest, context is very important to photojournalism, but also to portraiture. In *The Veteran Recalls*, the subject is the figure in near-profile, holding the flag with his gloved hand. There are some discernible elements to suggest who he is and what the occasion is. We can see that the subject himself is in uniform, but he is too old for active duty. We see that the other figures are older men. They carry flags on which each regiment's name is emblazoned over the French tricolor. The rows of people in identical chairs convey the idea of a meeting or ritual. The lines and lighting of the building suggest the men are in a large, old church. Many contextualizing items appear that convey solemnity and formality, but they are not quite enough to give the viewer the full idea. Without that context or a caption, the viewer's focus is thrown back onto the veteran in the foreground and his dignified, serious pose.

I wanted the photo to leave the viewer wondering what the service meant to the veteran, and what it meant to the veteran to be in a ceremony at which his service, decades in the past, was being called to active memory. I needed to frame him in a way that made him part of a unit, but also distinguishable as an individual having his own thoughts. The ceremony, held in the cathedral of Notre-Dame de Paris, was the 100th anniversary of the creation of France's veterans' services division.

Sometimes, choosing not to give the viewer much context can create a sense of mystery, anxiety, or excitement. The people in *Heart of the Beast* were a group of performers in a public show, held outdoors at night. They were dressed in cowls, and their makeup muted individual features. The torches they carried created a high-contrast lighting situation: the brightness of the fire "blew out" some tones in the image and plunged others into deep shadow. The scene was clearly not something one would see every day, and I wanted to heighten that sense as much as possible. The darkness robs the figures of any location context and renders them very small, but the fire they wield so emotionlessly makes them seem dangerous. The small figure to the far right of the frame, enshrouded so that only his or her face floats below the painted face raised aloft, gives no sense of what is being done in the scene or why. Thus, a very dramatic story unfolds in the image, and the viewer has only one tantalizing shard from which to assemble a whole.

◀ *The Veteran Recalls*   *Heart of the Beast* ▲

Narrative

A narrative is a story told to an audience. In a photographic medium, a narrative is "telegraphed" by compositional elements within the frame as well as by the style and technique used in shooting the subject. In many genres of photography (photojournalism, street, and travel photography, in particular), "telling a story" is a common, central feature.

Divining the narrative in a photo is sometimes quite subjective, especially if there are few contextualizing clues. A portrait may rely on the gestures or facial expression of the subject to project the subject matter. Style itself can be the story in a fine-arts photograph, if the technique is striking, such as in a photo featuring a high-contrast silhouette.

Etruscan Spouses, Rome, Italy, may seem prosaic and simple at first. This is a photo of an ancient sarcophagus in a museum (to the left and right you can see the glass boundaries of the case and, in the background, other glass cases with fluorescent lighting). The choice to photograph the case from the back, however, literally opens up a narrative. The Etruscan Sarcophagus of the Spouses in the Villa Giulia National Etruscan Museum in Rome features a deceased couple. The figure on the left places his affectionate arm around the shoulders of the figure to the right, and they share a gaze as they "look" out onto the corridor, reclining on their banquette.

Carabinieri, Siracusa, Sicily ▶
▼ *Etruscan Spouses, Rome, Italy*

Placing the camera behind the carved figures gives the illusion that the viewer shares their perspective, as though they were living and could see. The background has only a slight bokeh, so we have the telescoping effect of the corridor that narrows to a vanishing point (single-point perspective) in the near-center of the frame and of the cases of antiquities (Greek vases are partially visible) and silhouetted figures that recede into the distance.

Without a lot of artifice, a mood is created here, and the viewer is placed in a position to think about the viewpoint of this couple, dead for millennia. Ever since the museum put the sarcophagus on display a century ago, the couple has looked out on this static environment and, almost every day, living figures move before them like fleeting shadows.

The narrative suggested here could be a comment on the passage of time and the wish for eternal companionship. Nothing in the image requires the viewer to read one statement about one moment, as a photojournalist's image might, but the placement of the viewer behind the evocative, tender-looking couple is an invitation to imagine that couple's perspective on something humans cannot have: a sense of eternity.

Subject Matter

"Subject" and "subject matter" are often used interchangeably in common discourse, but an important distinction exists between the two terms in photography. The subject in a photo is defined by what is visibly in the frame with as little interpretation of its meaning as possible. The subject matter in a photo is the idea or mood or theme that the subject expresses and explores.

In *Carabinieri, Siracusa, Sicily*, then, you could say succinctly that the subject of the photo is two men standing, but that wouldn't give any insight into the photo's potential meaning. The subject matter of the photo is open to interpretation, but it could be "masculinity," or "friendship," or "silhouettes." Elements of style, genre, context of publication, and captioning are what will narrow the focus of possible subject matter.

To delve further into the subject matter of this photo, then, let's describe the compositional elements in play. The two figures are centered in the image, but they are in silhouette, so their identities are indeterminate. They wear hats, which suggest they are in uniform (cross-bands and epaulettes are also detectable on their clothing, suggesting a uniform). The photo is divided into thirds: the structure they're standing on occupies the bottom third, the figures are in the middle, and the sky (with a dark cloud) occupies the top third and drapes behind the men in the middle. All this makes the composition quite static.

The camera is positioned several feet below what would be eye-level with the figures. This camera angle, combined with the suggestion of uniforms, their assertive stances (it appears their arms are crossed in front of them and they are looking down or just over the photographer), and the severity of the contrast in the lighting all point to a style of photographing men that could come from film noir, socialist realism, or even fascist art. If "friendship" were on the table as a theme, it might be argued that little that is personal or relational is revealed about the figures: They lean toward each other but don't seem to be interacting significantly in the moment, and the anonymity granted by the deep shadow on their faces undermines the idea of an expression of strong personal feeling.

"Silhouettes" is an accurate description of how the elements in the frame are shot but, as subject matter, that doesn't get us much farther along than identifying the subjects. "Masculinity" is a better possibility, although that interpretation needs to be sharpened if it is to be descriptive—masculinity has many significant variations within the concept. The photographer's compositional choices—shooting the figures in harsh shadow; masking their faces to leave their confident stances and hints of a uniform as the viewer's only clues to identifying them; positioning the camera below the figures so they seem to loom over the viewer; and echoing artistic styles of framing men that emphasize impersonal male power—all contribute to making the subject matter of this photo "masculine authority."

If the photo appeared with a caption and a context, such as, "Sicilian Policemen on the Rim of an Ancient Greek Amphitheater," you, as a viewer, could refine your decisions about the image's subject matter. Does knowing the men's jobs and their setting change how you might think about their "masculine authority"? Does knowing they're standing on a crumbling ruin at sunset (just below the rim of the theater) add a more poignant comment on "masculine authority"? Why might a photographer want to withhold context or a caption from a viewer? Perhaps a photograph holds more artistic interest (such as if this photo were in an art gallery) if the viewer is less bound by additional input from the artist.

To read a photograph is to understand how its composition, technique, style, and subject are brought together to create subject matter for the viewer to react to. While it is true that viewers can have individual responses, and that artists can reflect personal meanings in their art that are important to them, a photograph in the public sphere is there to communicate an idea or condition. The tools of composition, technique, style, and subject create a connection between the image and its audience, much as words and grammar create a poem. Reception may vary somewhat, but the elements assert certain parameters of possibility.

Essentially, reading photos leads to you making well-reasoned decisions about an image's subject and subject matter—that is, who/what is the center of attention in the photo and what the photo has to say about the subject.

You have now covered several concepts essential to understanding photographic composition. You've looked at each of these concepts individually, and now is the time to learn how to coordinate them for a detailed and (I hope) enlightening analysis of images. Photographs are so rich in detail and resonances that absorbing the components that add up to an image's powerful impact can be difficult. Examining the parts that constitute the whole offers a chance to appreciate a stunning image even more; it allows you to see more than what a superficial, "overall" look will give you. A skilled photographer wants you to keep looking when you encounter an image. This chapter seeks to give you guidance in how to keep looking in such a way that your attention is rewarded and you are able to articulate what compels you in the photo.

In organizing the book, I arranged the vocabulary subjects in a descending scale of concepts from very broad to specific. The last topics in the vocabulary—subject matter, context, and narrative—are the most subjective and interpretive analytical tools. With them, you take the totality of what you've observed and decide what the photo is saying in its subject matter. Below, I will describe an organized approach to reading a photo for analysis, and then I will walk you through how to apply this to examples.

First Considerations—Introduction and Orientation

When first encountering an image, your first move toward understanding involves an overview of what is in the frame (and how putting the frame around the subject defines the image). Why did the photographer set up this particular boundary? How does the frame organize the subject? The framing introduces you to the subject and orients you to look at the elements in the frame with concentration.

Once you consider frame, look for the sharpest point of focus in the photo. It is highly likely that the sharpest point of focus in the frame is also the photo's focus, and that everything around that point of focus works toward compositional context. As you determine the focus in the photo, you can also assess the depth of field. Some images use small apertures (f8 and above) to maintain a clear focus throughout a good deal of the frame. If the depth of field seems particularly deep and broad, then it is a safe bet that the subject of the photo is broader than a single element in the frame.

Having assessed the focus and the depth of field, you can probably easily notice what element or elements in the frame have the most visual weight. What element has, in addition to the sharpest focus, the greatest tonal intensity, or the largest size, or the highest contrast from other items in the frame? The item with the most visual weight is an element that, once removed, would render the rest of the photo uninteresting or compositionally incoherent.

In *Armstrong Park, Louisiana*, the frame seems to bound much of a large Live Oak tree. The tree in the foreground touches, or nearly touches, every side of the frame. Parts of the tree are more sharply in focus than others. The depth of field in this image goes very deep, back through the arch created by the branches, all the way through to the house in the background. The house is only slightly out of focus in the background, but its contrast to the dark tree branches, and the framing they provide, calls attention to the house. Nonetheless, the oak in the foreground has an overwhelming visual weight because of its scale and its deep contrast with other elements in the frame. Most viewers could reasonably be expected to say, "That's a photo of a big tree."

▼ *Armstrong Park, Louisiana*

Second Considerations—Style and Technique

With these first considerations analyzed, we can next assess mood and genre through the use of style.

Turn your attention to the lighting in *Armstrong Park*. Is it high contrast, with strong darks and brights in the frame? Is it more diffused or tonally-balanced, so that the overall image seems more subdued or less dramatic?

Is there a key light or a backlight that calls attention to the subject in the frame or that leads to the point of sharpest focus? How important would you say lighting effects are to the composition of the image? In some cases in photography, the beauty of the light is the subject matter of the photo.

The perspective in a photograph is what leads your eye to particular elements in a frame first. Does the image have a single vanishing point, and does it lead you to the sharpest focus in the frame? Is there more than one vanishing point, leading the eye in different directions?

The camera angle works with perspective to guide your eye. Does the camera bring you close to the sharpest-focused or most strongly visually weighted element in the frame? Does it position you above it or below it? Do you feel you are connected or intimately close with the focal point, or do you feel at a remove? Are you a part of the action, or are you a voyeur?

Answering these questions, can you make a decision regarding what genre *Neptune Takes a Break, Barcelona, Spain*, falls into? Review

▲ *Neptune Takes a Break, Barcelona, Spain*

the information in the Genre chapter and make a decision about what type seems to fit. Once you name the genre of the photo, how does this affect how you interpret it?

The lighting in this photo is fairly even. Nothing appears to be in shadow, and the brights are not so strong that they stand out significantly. This fairly diffused, almost flat light allows the viewer to see everything in the frame at about the same level of intensity. The perspective in this photo seems to be parallel vanishing points, led by the railings around the tree. If you say the viewer's eye follows primarily a static, straight-on view, I could imagine an argument that there's a single vanishing point directly behind the central figure.

The camera angle is set just slightly above the subject—you can see the top of his head. The emphasis on the grass and the sidewalk as his backdrop (instead of perhaps sky or buildings) underscore this slight tilt downward to focus on him. The genre here appears to be either street photography or portraiture. I'd argue for street photography because the subject's self-presentation as a public performer is so prominent in regarding him. Moreover, he's clearly in an urban space. To be literal-minded about it, there's a street right behind him. Others, however, might say that portraiture is the stronger genre claim because the performer has been caught on a cigarette break, having a private moment in which his actual self is revealed.

Third Consideration—Specific Compositional Elements

Now we can get down to the structural details of the image—its composition. You probably have formulated some ideas about what is subject and what is subject matter in *The Walker of the Borders*. Compositional elements help you to make the case for your hypotheses about subject and subject matter.

Does the photo seem to have a hierarchy, such as a foreground or background, that directs you where to look? Where has the photographer placed the focal point in the photo—up close or farther away? What type of space does your eye have to travel through to see the subject?

Has the element with the most visual weight or sharpest focus fallen on one of the thirds in the Rule of Thirds? Or is the subject front-and-center in a more symmetrical composition?

What sort of ratio of scale is used in the image? Does the subject or chief focal element seem larger than life or minuscule? Is there a magnification of something usually insignificant, raising it to heightened importance, or does the subject seem to be rendered tinier and more distant than in your common experience? Is there a great contrast between elements in the frame, making one element far greater or smaller, closer or farther, higher or lower than another? Noticing scale may lead you to decisions not only about subject but also about subject matter because size can be a comment on importance or significance.

Do you see any leading lines in the photo? Do these lead you to or away from the subject, reflect the subject's gaze, or show you the subject's relationship to another object in the frame? Leading lines guide your eyes as they travel around the frame and, in doing so, they can give you clues about the story or theme a photo is presenting. What do you think the leading lines are doing in this photo?

Do you see an element in the photo that is framed by negative space? If so, there may be a use of figure-to-ground that calls attention to the subject. This can also be a manifestation of separation of subject. Does the focal figure seem to jump out from the image because of uncluttered space around it? Does a background recede behind the subject to the point that details of the subject seem unimportant or blurry? Does the image appear fairly consistently in focus across the frame, or is there significant bokeh, pulling one or more elements forward into focus while others recede because they are so hard to discern? How does any bokeh in the frame affect the focus and visual weight of your subject?

How close to realism do the elements in The *Walker of the Borders* seem? Can you detect elements that seem stretched, shrunken, overly heightened, or obscured? These distortions shape mood and attitude applied to the subject. How does distortion seem to call attention to some aspects of the subject?

The Walker of the Borders ▶

In this image, the foreground and background are fairly narrowly constrained. The only apparent leading line might be that of the sliver of sidewalk at the bottom of the frame—it traces out the likely path of the walker. The walker is just a foot or so in front of the garage, and he's slightly out of focus for all that he's in the foreground. He has just walked into the far-right third of the frame, and his approach to that third gives a more dynamic sense of motion in the image—you can imagine the trajectory of his walk across the frame, even though he's frozen mid-step. If he were shot at the moment t which he was framed in the center of the orange doors, the image would have a strong symmetrical elem eem more static—almost framed to the point of paralysis.

The scale here is a human scale because the camera is roughly at the same level as the subject's shoulder nat the viewer perceives him as being on the same level . The figure-to-ground is perhaps the main story The walker's white outfit and white hair stand out starkly against the bright blue wooden lap-siding. This ubject separation. As the only apparently animate figure in the frame, as well as being in the foreground subject" designation. The blue wall acts as negative space around him. There's strong color-blocking her oor, blue wall, and the all-white figure contrast sharply with each other, but they seem to all register with ity. The depth-of-field here is fairly shallow: everything seems more or less in focus, and there isn't an obv f bokeh at work in the photo.

Final Considerations—Subject Matter, Context, and Narrative

By this point in the analysis, you have a wealth of information about how your photo is framed, focused, structured, and styled. What does it all add up to for you? You can now make a well-supported case for the subject and likely subject matter of the photo: you know "who" or "what" and a great deal of "how," but the big pay-off in reading photos is your decision about "why"—why was the photo taken? Why are you being asked to pay attention to and think about what is in the frame?

Now, you're ready to ask and form credible answers to the questions of context and narrative.

In terms of narrative, what's the story in *The Gleaners*? How does the photographer use all the compositional elements and techniques to tell you this story? Who is this story about, and what is your relationship to this story? What do the style and technique tell you is the way to interpret this story?

Your (or the photographer's) implied relationship to the narrative can be found in clues about context within the frame, or in how the photograph points you to think about what's in the real world outside of the frame. Does the image place a subject in a context that you can recognize, read, or develop clues of meaning from? Or does the image give you an extreme close-up or isolated focus on the subject, offering details regarding a larger context (in or outside of the frame) that is very complicated? Does the narrative of the story suggest the subject matter—a symbolic or metaphoric interpretation of some real-world issue or idea? Where would you place the subject, subject matter, and narrative in the photo in the context of the real world or in the world of ideas? How does your evidence support this?

The Gleaners is a photo of several men involved in an event. The participants are captured in a tight enough frame that much context is lost. We can see they are dressed alike, implying a costume or uniform, and that they're all carrying sheaves of wheat. One scythe is partially revealed in the far left of the frame. We can see a wall and parts of a dwelling behind the figure, so they don't appear to be in the process of actual farming. We aren't given a clear view of any faces, so there's either mystery or anonymity in this story: the way the image is shot leads the viewer to identify them as a group rather than as individuals. The figure who dominates the frame in the foreground has his back to us, so we can see that he is obviously part of this group but can gather only faint cues about his age.

Without a single protagonist to focus on, the narrative seems to be about an event all of these people are sharing. They are oriented in roughly the same direction, united in costume and in the things they carry. We have enough context to suggest that a festival or parade is taking place, but the lack of definitive details leads us outside the photo to ask questions for greater context: What community are they a part of? What unites them? What are they celebrating? The narrative of this story leads mostly to a desire for more context, but the subject matter seems to leave us with a neutral or perhaps positive statement about unity and community. The context, given the tightness of the shot, is lacking in many details that would lead us to a definitive analysis. This is where a descriptive caption, such as, "Wheat Farmers' Coalition in Santa Marta Feast Day Procession," would fill in factual blanks and allow a thematic interpretation to be more focused.

Using this Vocabulary to Read a Photo

If you've followed all the steps for analysis in the preceding pages of this section, you have done the work that allows you to read a photo with more confidence in your understanding. You know how to use questions and answers to build an analysis, and you can convincingly argue for your interpretation. Let's now read a couple of photos together and build an analysis. Work through the checklist of considerations here, and then try the checklist on your own, going back through some of the photos that appeared earlier in the book. Remember, analysis and interpretation are skills, and they get better only with practice!

I've organized all the vocabulary according to the process outlined in "Putting It All Together." This checklist can give you an orderly, thorough method for analyzing an image.

◀ *The Gleaners*

PHOTO ANALYSIS CHECKLIST

A. INTRO AND ORIENTATION
1. Frame
2. Focus
3. Depth of field
4. Visual weight

B. TECHNIQUE AND STYLE
1. Lighting
2. Perspective
3. Camera Angle
4. Genre

C. COMPOSITIONAL ELEMENTS
1. Subject
2. Foreground/background
3. Rule of Thirds
4. Scale
5. Leading lines
6. Figure-to-ground
7. Negative space
8. Separation of subject
9. Bokeh
10. Distortion

D. CONCLUDING ANALYSIS
1. Context
2. Narrative
3. Subject matter

Example 1

Let's work through some photos together to give you practice reading photos with this guide. For the first example, we'll go through every item on the checklist.

INTRO AND ORIENTATION

1. What is in the frame of *Schmidt's Brewery, Saint Paul, Minnesota*? It's an old building, shot at night. In the frame is a large section of the building, filling most of the frame, and a cloudy night sky.

2. What is the focus of the photo? Much of the building is in focus, although the shot is dark and grainy. The lights on the building's signs and windows create sharp focus in several points in the frame. At three different points in the frame, the name of the building, "Schmidt's," is prominent and can be read clearly; two of these points are highly illuminated. Much of the building in shadow is fairly in-focus, but the darkness diminishes the sharpness.

Schmidt's Brewery, Saint Paul, Minnesota ▶

3. How is depth of field managed in the frame? Depth of field is fairly even and deep across the frame. The "Schmidt's" illumination in the right side of the frame is as in focus as the "Wash-" lettering in the foreground just below it.

4. What has the greatest visual weight in the frame? Though the smokestack to the left looms forward in the image, the brightly-lit "Schmidt's" tower to the right is wider and squatter and calls more attention to itself, locating the preponderance of visual weight there.

TECHNIQUE AND STYLE

1. What is the lighting situation in the photo? The lighting in this photo is dim, natural outdoor light (it is nighttime in the photo) and of points of bright artificial light at several points on the building—in windows and on illuminating signs. This creates a high-contrast situation of bright lights and dark shadows, much in the film noir style.

2. How is perspective used in this photo? This photo is shot from ground level, close to the building; the camera is focused close enough to the building for the subject to fill more than half

of the frame. This photo has three-point perspective: The smoke stack leads the eye to the upper first third of the frame; the lines to areas of the building from the left side and right sides of the frame at the bottom (the first floor of the building) lead the eye to a vanishing point in the dark corner on the bottom first third of the frame; the illuminated "Schmidt's" sign on the middle right of the frame leads the eye off the frame at the level of the right-hand bottom third point.

3. What is the angle of the camera in shooting this photo? This is a low-angle shot. The camera is placed at the ground-floor of the building (presumed, although the ground doesn't appear in the image), and tightly frames the structures in a way that makes the building seem to loom over the viewer, adding to its imposing air. There is a significant amount of keystoning because the camera is pointed at the building from an oblique angle.

4. What genre of photography does this image belong to? This image can be placed in any or all of several genres: It is a black-and-white photo. Its main subject is a building, which places it in the genre of architectural photography. The building

is an example of classic American Renaissance-style architecture, so this image could be seen as documentarian; given that the building is historically significant, this image could also be placed in the travel-photography genre. The high-contrast black-and-white lighting and the keystoning effect (the result of shooting the building with a wide-angle lens) give the photo a very stylized look, which might lead it to be categorized as fine-arts photography.

COMPOSITIONAL ELEMENTS

1. What is the subject of the image? The building is the only object in the frame. The sky behind and above lacks distinctive features.

2. What elements are in the foreground and background of the image? The foreground of the image is the first-through-third floors of the building, which are closest to the camera. The background of the image contains the smokestack, the tower, and the neon "Schmidt's" sign to the right, along with the sky. In this image, the illuminated background elements—the smokestack, tower, and neon sign—are more striking than the foreground imagery, and therefore the background dominates.

3. How does the Rule of Thirds play out in this image? The illuminated "Schmidt's" sign on the tower is situated at the intersection of the third horizontal third and the first vertical third. That placement, along with the sign's relative brightness, makes it the most arresting element in the frame. None of the other thirds contain an isolated, bright element.

4. How is scale deployed in the photo? The camera angle and filling of the frame in this image give the subject a monumental scale. The structure fills the frame, occupying the fore-, middle-, and background of the photo. The keystoning effect generated by the wide-angle lens distorts the subject, creating the impression that the smokestack and tower are bending toward the center of the frame and leaning away from the viewer, even as they appear to loom from above. This makes the building seem massive.

5. Are there leading lines in the frame of the photo? There are several. The smokestack, tower, turrets, and exhaust pipe (center) act as vectors that lead the eye up the building and toward the sky at the top of the frame, creating an impression that the building is soaring. The jutting corner of the building in the center of the frame also acts as a leading line, causing the eye to travel up the building. The unbroken white lines along the top of the first floor of the building (which frame the marquee-lit signs) terminate in a dark corner at the bottom-left part of the frame. The neon sign causes the eye to travel off the image to the middle-right. The overall effect is an Escher-like geometric maze within the image.

6. Are any elements in the frame situated in a strong figure-to-ground relationship? The smokestack and the tower are grounded strongly against the featureless sky—the tower more powerfully so because its lighting provides a higher contrast.

7. How is negative space employed in the photo? The night sky acts as negative space in one-third to one-half of the photo, isolating the building and making it the sole focus of the image.

8. Is there strong separation of subject in the image? Yes. As a result of the framing of the subject against a contrasting, monolithic background, the subject stands out clearly.

9. Is bokeh a feature of this photo? No, in this case, the background is featureless, so there is no sense of blur in the image.

10. Is distortion at work in this image? Yes. The wide-angle lens bends the smokestack and tower strikingly. As a result, they are not at right-angles in the image; because of this keystoning effect, the building simultaneously seems to be leaning away from the viewer and collapsing into the center of the photo.

CONCLUDING ANALYSIS

1. What context do you have or need for understanding this photo's subject matter? The photo includes several signs that give the viewer an idea of what this building is. The name "Schmidt's" occurs several times on the building's facade and is key-lit or self-illuminated in three places. One of the marquee-lit places at the bottom of the photo reads "Brew-House." With these clues as context, an inquisitive viewer could identify this building as the Schmidt's Brewery factory in Saint Paul, Minnesota. The style of the building marks it as American Renaissance, so we understand that this building is over 100 years old. Beyond that, nothing discernible is happening around or within the building, so we have no context for thinking that this photo is about anything other than the building itself. The only alternative for subject matter is the style and manner of the shooting, which underscore the structure's antique design.

2. Now that you've examined the image thoroughly for its technique, style, and compositional elements, what narrative can you discern in the photo? This photo takes on a seemingly inert subject—a century-old building—and places it at the center of the frame. The dramatic style of the image, however, makes this photo of a building seem to be about more than documentarian, "straight" photography. The high-contrast, film noir, black-and-white technique, coupled with distortion from a wide-angle lens, makes this photo seem to be projecting mood for the viewer of the image.

3. What is the subject matter of the image? Because the building is presented without context, and there appears to be no action or living entity to be interpreted in the frame, we are left to contemplate the building itself, which leaves the subject matter open to analysis of style or subject for the subject's sake. The most striking feature of the building seems to be its vintage architecture, and the black-and-white tonal choice enhances the historical sense of the building by drawing on the idea of black-and-white photography as the marker of an old photo. One could say, then, that the subject matter of the photo is the age and style of the building or the mood evoked by the lighting and style elements that surround the subject.

Example 2

Now let's use the checklist on a somewhat more complicated photo.

INTRO AND ORIENTATION

1. What is in the frame of this photo? *Ponte Gobbo, Bobbio, Italy*, is framed in the background by the sky and two large hills. In the foreground, the photo is bounded by what appears to be a gate post on the bridge on the left; on the right, the edge of the town and the bridge's wall appear. At the bottom of the photo, the image is bounded by the road-bed of the bridge.

2. What is the focus of the photo? The focus of the photo appears to be the church at the end of the bridge, but there is also a small running figure in focus on the bridge just before the church.

3. How is depth of field managed in the frame? The depth of field in this photo goes deep, but is not consistent throughout the entire frame. The foreground, in the bottom-third of the frame, is slightly out of focus. The mountains and sky in the background are somewhat out of focus due to atmospheric perspective. The middle-third of the frame is in the sharpest focus—there, you can see the second half of the bridge, the runner, some other pedestrians, and the first line of buildings of the town.

4. What has the greatest visual weight in the frame? The angled path of the bridge is highest in contrast and sharpest in focus; the running figure is highlighted because she appears almost completely framed by the leading-line of the bridge's pavement. The church has a great deal of visual weight: It is in-focus, is vertical among horizontal objects, and is in relatively high contrast to its surroundings. In addition, the leading lines of the hill profiles seem to point to it.

112

TECHNIQUE AND STYLE

1. What is the lighting situation in the photo? This image was shot in diffused natural light. There are neither harsh shadows nor obvious directional lighting.

2. How is perspective used in this photo? The hills and the trajectory of the bridge encourage viewing this photo as having a single-point perspective, although the road at the end of the bridge does imply lines leading off to the left and (more strongly) the right of the frame.

3. What is the angle of the camera in shooting this photo? The angle of the camera appears to be an eye-level long shot. This is complicated a bit by the dip of the bridge: the camera is above that in-focus part of the frame. At the same time, because the church building is far away, it appears to be on the same level as the camera sensor.

4. What genre of photography does this image belong to? This image contains buildings and a bridge that are distinctly European and pre-modern in style, and none of the human figures are large enough to be the main subject of the photo. The natural elements and small-town elements compromise the image as street photography, and there's not enough distinctive or active about the piece to place it firmly in the photojournalism or documentarian categories. Though the photo does not focus too strongly on the buildings themselves, the architectural style seems to be the photo's strongest element, and this image fits best in the travel-photography genre.

Ponte Gobbo, Bobbio Italy ▶

COMPOSITIONAL ELEMENTS

1. What is the subject of the image? While the church, its town setting, and the running figure all call attention to themselves, the bridge itself is the dominant element in the frame.

2. What elements are in the foreground and background of the image? The foreground of the photo is the slightly out-of-focus end of the bridge. The background contains a small European town with mountains and sky framing it.

3. How does the Rule of Thirds play out in this image? The center is emphasized more strongly than the thirds in this image, although the slight jog that the bridge takes to the left begins in the bottom middle third, and the bell towers of church terminate in the top middle third. The effect is to make the eye feel that it is traveling "deep" into the center of the image.

4. How is scale deployed in the photo? In this photo, the emphasis on far-away elements has the effect of miniaturizing them—the town and the human figures are tiny. However, the path of the bridge starts at human scale, or even slightly larger, and diminishes to the vanishing point, shrinking the bridge as well.

5. Are there leading lines in the frame of the photo? The leading line of the bridge's path dominates the photo. The fact that the line is not straight makes the line seem more dynamic because it causes the eye to traveling in more than one direction.

6. Are any elements in the frame situated in a strong figure-to-ground relationship? The bridge's center is in bright contrast to the river bed on either side of it. The running figure is grounded by being centered in the left-hand strip of concrete on the bridge. The bell towers contrast somewhat to the sky and clouds.

Serpent and Friend, Cocullo, Italy ▶

7. How is negative space employed in the photo? The largest amount of negative space in the photo is the sky, which acts as a backdrop to the town.

8. Is there strong separation of subject in the image? If the bridge path itself is the subject, the path is separated strongly from other elements at all points in the frame, in part because the walls give it a distinct, consistent border.

9. Is bokeh a feature of this photo? Bokeh is not a significant feature of the photo. While the foreground is slightly out of focus, it does not appear to be a major aesthetic element in the frame.

10. Is distortion at work in this image? There is slight distortion in the foreground of the image, but the majority of the image is realistically rendered.

CONCLUDING ANALYSIS

1. What context do you have or need for understanding this photo's subject matter? The architecture itself is the chief context element for the subject—it is a medieval town with a medieval bridge. Because this photo seems to fall best into the travel-photography genre, more satisfying context would come from knowing the precise location and some history of the bridge and town.

114

2. Now that you've examined the image thoroughly for its technique, style, and compositional elements, what narrative can you discern in the photo? Bridges symbolically suggest connections but, in this photo, the length of the bridge from the photographer to the town is striking. Because of this, the narrative seems to be about the tenuousness of connecting to something so far away; even if the pathway is clearly marked, it must be traversed.

3. What is the subject matter of the image? The bridge's path is framed in order to emphasize its length and deviating path. This makes the town and the figures in the center of the image appear even smaller and more distant than they might if the photographer had cropped out the bottom-third, out-of-focus part of the image, even without changing the focal length of the lens. The distance and the leading lines are the story here. That actual distance from the medieval town, combined with the antiquating effect of black-and-white photography, works metaphorically to suggest that the subject matter is the distance of the past from the photographer and viewer, with the bridge offering the tantalizing possibility that the goal can be reached.

Example 3—Short Form

You've seen the "long-form" of using this checklist. It is useful for an academic study of a photograph and also for examining photographic technique in detail if you wish to develop your own skills as a photographer. Once you've practiced on enough examples that you've gained confidence in your ability to recognize the concepts and spot them in an image, you needn't use the checklist exhaustively to analyze photos.

Let's try a short-form version of the checklist to read a photograph. You may want to work on this as practice for explaining how a photo works more briefly, as if you were developing a gallery or museum card for it or wanted to communicate the substance of the photo to a non-professional audience.

Because of the central focus, the shallow depth of field, the close-up angle, and the high-key lighting, the dominant subject of this image (*Serpent and Friend, Cocullo, Italy*) is clearly the snake in the foreground and the hand holding it. This photo doesn't strongly employ the Rule of Thirds: the subject is centered, but the eye of the snake is on the upper horizontal third. The background is rendered as bokeh but not so fully that you can't see the context of the subject. The frame contains the brightly-contrasting apparel of the person holding the snake, and, in the background behind her, other people are clearly gathered at an event, though they are rendered in a soft but recognizable degree of bokeh. The snake, because it is so strongly foregrounded and shot in close-up, is presented in a scale that makes it seem larger than real life. There aren't many strong leading lines in the photo, except for the stripes along the body of the snake, which lead the viewer's gaze to the snake's head. The red sweater of the snake handler acts as a strong ground for the figure of the snake and also provides strong separation of the subject from its background. The separation of subject is stronger on the left of the snake than the right because the contrast of red to gold is stronger than cream to gold. The narrative of the photo is a bit hard to determine—it could be a study in the contrast between the texture of the snake's skin and the hand of its holder. The festive colors of the holder, and the glitter on her nails, combined with the people in the background who are warmly greeting each other, suggest that this is a public social event. And, indeed, it is not every day that someone walks around holding out a live snake for others to photograph. These clues imply that the subject matter of the photo is the dramatic, colorful festivities of a local holiday, which places this photo in the travel or street-photography genre. The snake is in atypical, urban surroundings so, although it is a creature that is at home in nature, its location far from home rules the photo out as nature photography. The snake dominates the image, which means that the person holding the snake can't be said to be represented in a portrait—too little of her is in focus to make her personality a strong component within the frame.

Example 4—Short Form

Performing the "short form" analysis can give you a relatively quick answer to why a photo "works" the way it does.

In *The Blue Man, Guthrie Theater, Minneapolis, Minnesota*, three physical elements are discernible: the building, a man's head, and the sky. All three of these elements are framed to appear partial—there's no perspective on the sky to indicate whether it's a clear or cloudy day or what time of day it might be; the building is rendered as a fragment (it is obviously a modern construction, but too little context is provided to say what the building is; the man is at a distance from us and in profile, so the image can't be said to be a strong portrait of an individual. The focus within the frame is consistent throughout—the man is slightly less sharp than the much larger building, and the sky is featureless, acting as a negative space. So the depth-of-field cannot be said to be a deciding factor in determining the subject. The building is darker and larger than the man's head, so it carries a lot of visual weight, but its structure acts to frame the man's head in the center of the image, and that causes the head to be more visually compelling. The building is on a monumental scale compared to the man, nearly creating another kind of negative space, like the sky. The building and the sky act as a frame-within-a-frame, and create a strong figure-to-ground relationship with the man's head. The contours of the building act as both vertical and horizontal leading lines, pointing to the head as the only element in the composition that is round rather than angular. The camera is angled several feet below the man's head, which makes the figure seem more remote and almost abstract. Because the depth-of-field is so uniform, and the sky is so blank, there isn't much sense of a foreground or background, and this contributes to making this photo feel seem to fit more in the genre of abstract photography, even though it is composed of architecture and a human figure. The blue tonal range and muted lighting of the entire image also create a sense of unreality. The fragmentation of the building and the man discourage a reading of this photo as documentarian or architectural. The composition is so static that it is hard to sense a narrative in the sense of a story with plot elements. The subject matter may be the compelling geometry of the image, calling for it to be considered fine-arts photography. For some viewers, the modernist architecture and emotionless, remote person dwarfed in the frame might evoke a story of alienation in modern life. I chose to caption this image *The Blue Man* to allow for both of these interpretations—the arts-photography viewpoint with the literal blueness of the figure and the emotional connotation of "feeling blue" in English.

As you can see from these examples, once you've mastered the terms, you can provide a concise but thorough analysis of a photo in a single paragraph, using almost all of the terms. The goal of the checklist to read a photo is to use the most pertinent of the vocabulary to provide a focused and coherent analysis. It's a good idea to search the photo for all of these concepts but, in your final analysis, you can center on the ones that best support your interpretation.

Blue Man, Guthrie Theater, Minneapolis, Minnesota ▶

CONCLUSION: NEXT STEPS

You now have a range of tools and an orderly approach for observing photos more closely and deriving a more satisfying understanding from them. If you are a student of photography as an art form, you can carry this guide with you to practice reading photos in galleries, museums, books, and daily life, with the aim of developing your own taste. You're now able to discover and articulate why particular artists or styles of photography appeal to you. You'll understand better, too, how and why some photos, especially in advertising and politics, have such a powerful impact on you and other viewers. Your next steps may be to look more often, or more deeply, at photos that make an impression on you. You may want to start looking at collections of famous photographers or attending art shows of photography that might before have made you feel uncomfortable or bored. When you look at various professional photographs, spend a little time comparing uses of framing, the Rule of Thirds, or visual weight. Start seeing distortion and bokeh. Be curious about the narrative a photo or a series of images might be telling.

If you are an aspiring photographer, a worthwhile use of this book would be to start looking critically at your own photos. Not so much "critically" in the sense of deciding whether your photos are good or bad, but in the sense of paying attention to how you construct your images. What are your favorite subjects? What camera angles do you feel most interested in using? What techniques haven't you tried, but you'd like to? You might set yourself up with exercises in which you approach one subject from different camera angles, or expose it in different kinds of lighting, or recompose your frame by changing up scale, or use leading lines or figure-to-ground. Every one of the concepts we have used here is an opportunity to experiment with your existing skills and to expand your abilities. People often think the best way to improve their photography is to buy equipment—new, better, more. Such tools can be wonderful, but there is no substitute for consciously improving your technique.

The poet William Butler Yeats wrote, "The world is full of magic things, waiting for our senses to grow sharper." I hope this book has helped you to improve your senses, and that you will observe (and photograph!) more of the magic things that await you.

Acknowledgements

I wish to thank my husband and colleague, Professor Robert Gremore, for the innumerable hours he spent talking with me about photography, watching me take photos, enduring me photographing him, and cheering me on as I wrote this book. His fine company, good nature, and excellent eye have made me better at everything I do. "... all the gardens I have ever gazed at, longing."

    I also want to thank Wendell Ricketts at FourCats Press for his incomparable editing and unflagging encouragement. *"E quindi uscimmo a riveder le stelle."*

Contact Carolyn Whitson through her online portfolio at https://www.madmaenad.com.

Also by Carolyn Whitson

This introduction to the themes and conventions of Last Judgment art in the Middle Ages is designed for both the beginning student and the traveler and will orient both to the paintings, carvings, and mosaics that, at first glance, may seem overwhelming in their complexity. Organized according to prominent figures that appear in the genre—Christ in Majesty, Archangel Michael, Satan, angels and demons, the Saved, and the Damned—this study explains character, symbols, gestures, and actions with reference to medieval conventions and to religious texts and traditions. The pre-Christian origins and influences of some recurring characters, such as Satan, are also examined. The 70 detailed photos of medieval artworks from Spain, France, and Italy allow readers to get closer to the art than they would in real life, and the text introduces and illuminates the visual and iconographic vocabulary of art history and religion not usually explained by museum placards.

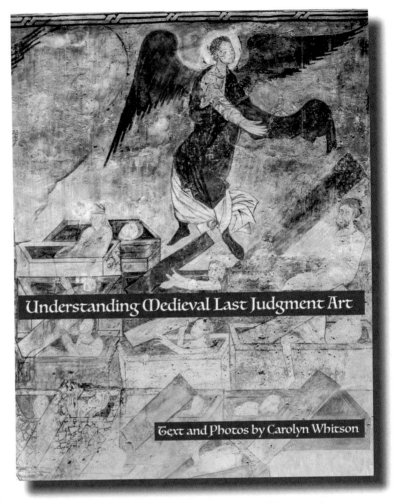

Understanding Medieval Last Judgment Art
70 color photographs; 109 pages
Available in paperback & for Kindle readers
ISBN-13: 978-1690654667

Made in the USA
San Bernardino, CA
09 January 2020